MASTER
YOUR
UNIVERSE

ALSO BY GARY STUART

Many Hearts, One Soul

God Says, Heal!

Gems of Inspiration

2004: Nature of the Beast

WITH TRACY REPCHUK

Empower Business Everywhere

MASTER YOUR UNIVERSE

How To
Direct & Star
In Your Own Life

GARY STUART

ISBN-13: 978-1518810688
ISBN-10: 1518810683

I dedicate this book to the many wonderful clients who have shared their "family home movies" with me. Together, we have accessed the seemingly lost footage of the past, and given voice to the silent movie playing beneath their real life dramas and traumas.

As always, they were the directors of their own pictures. I was merely an associate director asking them to look at key scenes and leave the rest on history's cutting room floor.

It has been my honor to sit in and help with the rewriting of these scripts so that their messages empower us all to see our family's story in a different light.

CONTENTS

FOREWORD

by
Robert Clancy

I t is a true pleasure and honor to share with you the work of my friend and colleague Gary Stuart. Gary is not only a master Trans-Generational Constellation Facilitator, Author, Teacher and Speaker but he's someone I've come to know as a true healer of the human spirit.

Healing is so much more than just the physical aspect. True health involves everything — your mind, body and spirit. Occasionally life places us into a nasty storm, and it's okay to duck for cover during these trials. All storms eventually pass and the skies return to blue when the sun shines down upon us again. This is the critical time when you need to face the devastation left behind by that storm to start your rebuilding process. When you rebuild, there is always an opportunity to make things better than they were before. This is where you can take charge to direct your outcome.

As Gary clearly describes in this remarkable book, we can become the stars of our own lives. Each of us has the ability to direct our destiny, change our life scripts, and rewrite our endings. He shares how our role in life is a choice, and *Master Your Universe* is about realizing our true potential.

Personal empowerment is the key, and Gary shows how Constellation Healing unlocks the subconscious door to the difficulties that block us along the way.

As I read through the pages of this book, I was struck by the fact of how easy it is for me to implement these concepts in my own life. I'm confident you will find the same in the wisdom contained on these pages.

On a final note, I've actually had the honor of participating in one of Gary's Constellation Healings while I was on a retreat for the Evolutionary Business Council in Vancouver. It was there I experienced firsthand how much Gary cares about others. If you want to see the most beautiful gifts this world has, just witness how Gary opens another's heart with kindness and healing and you will know them all.

Know that every peaceful sunrise is born to shine upon your beautiful heart. Every wave in the ocean is meant to flow over your precious soul. Every star in the universe shines for your loving spirit — and you're that star! I wish you true peace and healing on your journey. Now is time to write true happiness into your life!

Love & Light,
Robert Clancy
Author of *The Hitchhiker's Guide to the Soul*

PREFACE

Everything you see, hear, smell or touch becomes part of your experience of life as a picture stored in your memory. Every day you are alive, your senses capture millions of images, sounds, thoughts, feelings, and impressions. These thousands of images or frames transform into fast moving pictures that become the "Movie Of Your Life". Over time, many of these stored memories are compressed. Imagine having a movie of your life made in two hours. The major moments are paramount to the story and are featured in the scenes on the screen.

You already are the star of your own Life. You act and react to life as it unfolds on a daily basis. Actors follow scripts and can change some of the words of the script, but they do not have overall influence on the direction of the movie itself. The goal of *Master Your Universe* is to inspire you to harness and empower yourself in every aspect of your life. You can become more than just the star. You can write and direct the movie too.

The universe of possibility presents itself to you daily. There is enormous potential for change. As the screenwriter and director, you can influence your life in any direction you would like it to go. You also have influence over the main character — his or her motivations, history, and inspiration. Your past is carried forward into who you are today. If your past was a movie like *Psycho* or *Natural Born Killers*, the present and future would be heavily influenced by the drama. However, what if you could change the movie to end like *It's A Wonderful Life*? Perhaps then you could imagine how "the Force would be with you."

I want to inspire you to be proactive in creating your current and future memories in a powerful way. After all, the stakes are high and production can shut down at any time. The time is now to "Master Your Universe." Learn to see exactly how your ancestral history shapes your current reality and how that reality can be changed by exploring the backstory behind your family movie. It may have more influence on you than you think.

I believe that you will be transformed by hidden things you thought you knew but you did not see. This spacious present is your opportunity to rewrite the past to create a blockbuster future. That is what every director and star wants. My hope is that this book will help you realize how your life is like a movie, a vehicle to get your name to the top of the theater marquee, starring you as the "Master of Your Universe."

Gary Stuart
Studio City, California, 2015

PART ONE

The STORY

1.
SOUL MISSION:
THE MOVIE OF YOUR LIFE

At the beginning of this incarnation there was a very specific intention or mission which was preset for your journey from spirit to physical. It is possible that during your formative years your family system distracted you from that intention but still you needed your family to survive and grow into adulthood. The fact is that they nurtured you and taught you the ways of the world so that you could carry your soul mission into adulthood.

Constellations give you a way to explore and reconnect with your original soul mission. It's a process that helps you rediscover who your really are and what you came here to do. After all, you are a separate, autonomous, spiritual being seeking the best human experience possible. It is your universe and now you get to create the future that fulfills you.

We start backstage in the spiritual realm with an intention for what we want to experience. We set the conditions to manifest a "Soul Mission" and to make the "Movie" of our creation. Even unseen forces that seemed against us only strengthen our resolve.

As a child we were an actor or actress in our parents'

movies as well. Our birth was a message to the world of infinite possibilities for happiness and fulfillment. We may not want to think we are an actor in our life. However, as Shakespeare said, "All the world's a stage." Some of you like to charge and direct. Others take pride in being in supporting roles. Neither is good or bad, it is just what you have chosen for this lifetime. There is one saving grace. You have hidden behind the scenes the most empowering role you could have — the role of the editor. You have the power to change your story, alter its direction, create a new version of your character, delete scenes, and reshape the plot. You can transform the outcome through your creative interpretation.

If a story or situation does not serve you, cut it out or snip the parts that you do not like. Use your hindsight to make the past be what you want it to be. At the very worst you'll end up with a hysterical blooper reel or slap stick screwball comedy of errors. Isn't it better than having a grief stricken drama? Just cut it out and leave it on the cutting room floor.

Looking at your life through the lens of a Constellation gives you a rare glimpse and multidimensional view of the original cast of characters commonly known as your family. As we all know things were not always as they seemed. There may have been a deeper, more mysterious plot line occurring as you acted out your part or role within your family system. Every other family member was also acting out the scenarios that they needed so they could learn their own lessons.

Both positive and negative experiences could happen simultaneously. One family member could see something as positive and another could see it as negative. It is a matter of perception and what story that individual made up about the experience. Constellations give you a wider perspective so you can see the whole picture. In a Constellation you can see the bigger forces at work creating dramas and traumas in your family. You get to watch objectively and see it from a different perspective. You can free yourself from the past.

After all it is the movie of your life. It will continue to unfold. The question is, do you want it to continue in the same manner which it has been or do you want to alter it? You have the power to change your beliefs. Choose to let go of footage that does not work. Change the scenes to be empowering instead. It is your choice. The feature film remains eternally yours as the movie is your life and your life is the movie.

2.

HOW YOUR LIFE STORY SUPPORTS YOUR MOVIE

Everyone has a life story. You have one plan for how you want it to go, life may have another. It seems to be a manifestation of some script we are following unbeknownst to us as life unfolds. Are we along for the ride or creating the ride? It seems sometimes that both are true. You can be supported by life or victimized by the negative circumstances. Each has its own reward or price. As a child you may have felt others were in charge. Your well-being was in their hands. You may have been subjected to abuse, often by someone in your own family. Where do you turn when your creators and protectors are against you? Many people go within to protect themselves. Such people have deep reserves of strength, tenacity, and loyalty that help them stay alive and thrive at all costs. However sometimes negative scenes seem to stand out because they were so unpleasant. They are not easily forgotten.

Your movie may have progressed forward from negative scene to negative scene. Or it could have had many positive scenes with a just few negative ones thrown into the mix. No matter which, we all reach adulthood with some baggage we pick up along the way. The paradox is that the negatives create resolve within us. They are tests to strengthen us so we can endure adversity. Life teaches us well so we can survive and thrive like the character of George in *It's A Wonderful Life*.

If we see the scenes from the past as too overwhelming and get lost, our spirit can be crushed. Those who don't resolve these issues may replay the victim story again and again or act out, becoming a perpetrator who causes harm to others. Our movie might degenerate into something like *Silence of the Lambs*. Ironically life itself does not seem to prefer one over the other. We see this in ancient fables as well everyday news.

Becoming a conscious being allows you to live from the perspective of presence, making smarter choices from each moment to the next. It is an adventure into the unknown. There is a short window of time to create your adventure and legacy before the credits roll. Your family will be able to learn from your new insights as well.

Follow along and see what happens when you decided to master your universe. How exciting to direct and star in your own movie. Bravo, kudos, and congratulations for taking this journey. The curtain is rising. Come in and enjoy your show.

Lights, Camera, Action. It's Showtime!

3.

STAR POWER

Whether you know it or not, you have been consciously and unconsciously writing your "Life Story" all along. Now that you are choosing to direct and be the star, you must take responsibility for the script, supporting actors, location and plot. This is your movie. It is time to take action and create the movie that you want your life to be in a way that serves your fate and destiny the best. It is your name on the marquee. Manifest your vision and build your own personal legacy that your audience will love. Then your legacy will live on long after you've exited stage left. In Los Angeles, people still bring fresh flowers to the grave sites of film stars Rudolph Valentino and Marilyn Monroe even though it's been over 50 years since they passed on. That is a true legacy. That is how to star and wow an audience so much they honor you long after your death.

What is your "Star Power?" Most stars know their strengths and weaknesses. They play to their strengths. What are your strengths? Here are some to consider: your wisdom, spiritual awareness, looks, personality, wit, inventiveness, tenacity, choices, wardrobe, supporting cast, ideas, likability, humor, and emotions. While adjectives are a good place to start, always know you are so much more than a list. Know what makes you stand out as a lead actor in your life movie. One key is to find the right vehicle; the job or career that helps you express and utilize your unique personality strengths, and skill set.

Which genre suits you best? Is your movie a classic, action adventure, tragedy, comedy, drama, tearjerker, documentary or a horror film? Which vehicle serves you to cultivate your star power? You are the director so you need to know which genre serves you and your talents the best.

Maximize and orchestrate all the elements that you need to have in place for you to skyrocket to the top of your game. If what you have planned is any good, the audience will support you and cheer you on. If not, they will actually direct you to make some edits and cause you to reflect on making some plot changes. The audience is made up of the people in your life. You are part of their universe as they are a part of yours. You all support each other's movie. Not only are you smack in the middle of your own movie, you have chosen to be an "Extra" in other people's movies too.

Have you ever noticed how many movies you have seen where you don't even remember what happened? What is most interesting about this "video-amnesia" is that the lead actors may be etched into your memory forever even if it has been decades since you have seen the film. That is "Star Power!" They outshine the film whose title you can't even remember and stay alive in the screen of your memory.

In a similar way, there are certain scenes from your life or scenes from your family that you focus on. You are not aware of the overall picture or movie, just the scenes that replay over and over in your mind. These scenes affect your everyday life. It is important to step away from these scenes and understand the bigger picture. It is time to get on with it because life is short. Do not water down your dreams or expectations.

Now let's think about the title of your life's movie. Here are some movie titles for inspiration. See if one of them is a good title for your life script or make up one of your own:

- *From Here To Eternity*
- *Terms Of Endearment*
- *Superman*
- *Thelma & Louise*
- *Rocky*
- *All About Eve*
- *The Lost Weekend*
- *A Streetcar Named Desire*
- *Ghost*
- *Back to the Future*
- *Silence of the Lambs*
- *The Miracle Worker*
- *Braveheart*
- *Schindler's List*
- *American Beauty*

As you ponder this, think about why you relate to it. You are the director. You are the star. You can take control and even edit it. Transform the concept. Alter the plot to create the movie you want. Live it, support it and breathe it into existence.

4.

BEHIND-THE-SCENES

The process of Constellations is a multidimensional window into the backstory of your life and all of the people in your family who came before. It is like a retro black and white silent picture hiding in the background behind your current 3D live action reality. Most often this other silent film is laced with unresolved historical issues like tragedy, trauma, and frozen emotions especially grief and shame. Typically the backstory is fraught with betrayal, drama, incest, murder, accidents, intrigue, and secrets. Most people do not want to speak about what happened or be honest about the family secrets. They often don't even know what happened in the past and would prefer not to know. The hidden, toxic and dysfunctional stories were sanitized or swept under the rug to protect the family name and reputation. Got shame?

The biggest misconception is that the truth will hurt more than the lies meant to protect. Ironically it is the deception that does the real damage. Deception that lingers for many generations beyond the time of the original misfortune. These negative dynamics can last for centuries. It may seem like an exercise in futility to explore ancient family history but I guarantee you it's not! Even though some of these people died long before you were born, their destiny and fate reside in your own body's DNA. Their drama and trauma continue to roll forward from generation to generation, doomed to continue to repeat until it's revealed and resolved. The long historical, ancestral bloodline casts its shadow in your life. Don't forget: You are their future as they are your past.

Constellation Healing is a actually a very efficient way to replay the movie of your ancestors and thereby reveal to you in the present what happened in the past. You get to have an historical window into their lives, a tremendous opportunity to excise whatever toxic energy hides in your family system as well as appreciate whatever skills, strength, and resourcefulness they used to survive. During a Constellation Healing you watch the historic events unfold before your eyes like you are watching a movie. You get to replay/revisit unfinished scenes until they are healed. Important people in your family are represented by audience members, let's call them the "actors". They intuitively voice what needs to be said to clear what made them feel "stuck" in the roll, thereby releasing the energy of the traumatic event.

Imagine your family is a series of Russian nesting dolls. You are one doll outside the doll of your parents. They are outside the doll of their parents. Each generation is the next doll in line. Their lives have an effect on yours. Lessons pass down from parents to children.

Constellations give us a front row seat into the "Theater of the Absurd" that is contained within our family systems, a live opportunity to let the past unfold and be completed. Our subconscious is made conscious. Hidden truths are spoken, toxic energies are set free. This also liberates us from physical tension contained within our bodies and our DNA where the ancestral past has an energetic hold. If you question whether or not this could be true, look at multigenerational disease and chronic health conditions in your family of origin. These can be the shadow of unresolved ancestral historical experiences contained and stored biologically in your family.

Look at a Constellation Healing Experience as a *Back to the Future* opportunity that awakens you from *The Twilight Zone*, giving you your individual freedom and personal empowerment at warp speed. It can be faster than you can say "Beam me up, Scottie." "The Force" can awaken within you just as it did in Luke Skywalker. All kidding aside, that "other" dimension is real. You have the power in the present to change the direction of your whole ancestral lineage. Changing the way you perceive and understand the past affects your present. You have the power to make this happen. So on with the show!

5.

MOVING BEYOND
YOUR STORY

Most of what happened in our lives has served us. While we view some events as positive and some as negative, more often than not we belabor the negative much more than necessary and minimize the positive. Regardless of what happened, you lived to tell the tale. So that's good. Now you know your story inside out, outside in, backwards and forwards and backwards again. The biggest question is:

Why can't we let go of the past?

Why do we hold onto what does not serve us? What is the secondary gain? Do we crave pity? Does a "poor me, poor me" attitude serve anyone? Traumatic events do cause pain and anguish. We don't want to minimize their negative aspects. However, have you ever noticed some people seem to get some self-righteous kick talking endlessly about how they were victimized by parents, siblings or schoolyard bullies? What's going on here?

Why do bad things happen? Is it life testing us, pushing

us to stand up for ourselves? To find the strength to say "No more!" "Take this job (abuse, bad marriage, war, illness, and all the other junk) and shove it?" Remember that:

Adversity makes us strong.

This fact of creation applies not just to humans but also to insects, animals, mammals and even phytoplankton. Life can push us to our limit. As in *Survivor,* it's a reality show. Our goal is to discard the roll of playing the victim, reframe the struggles of the past, and acknowledge the powerful life force flowing through in everything and everyone. After all,

We made it.
We passed the test.
We survived.
Can you we be happy now?
If not, why?

Life is a continually shifting dance of events. We determine how these events affect us. We can shift our perception and quit mindlessly repeating toxic patterns. When the fog of the past is cleared we can create fresh new patterns that better serve us, our families, and the whole world.

6.

SELF-HEALING
EXERCISES

Events from your past affect us in the present. This includes both positive and negative experiences such as when we feel victimized. Take out a blank piece of paper and list the following:

1. Five positive ways your past has helped you. Include the people involved.

2. Five negative ways letting go of the past would hurt you.

3. Five events where you felt victimized in any way by any person or persons including family members. Include the people involved.

4. Five ways you overcame being victimized.

Reflect on the following question: Would you be the same person today if these events — whether you determine them to be good or bad — did not happen?

Look at the lists you wrote. Identify those people who affected you negatively. One by one imagine each person right in front of you. You are yourself in the current moment. Even if the negative event happened when you were a child, you are doing this in current time. Thank each of those people. See them as a teacher that life sent your way to test your mettle.

Bow to each person or to the situation. It was a gift and now you can see it for what it was. Thank each person for helping you to become strong. They are responsible for their actions. Let them carry what is theirs instead of you carrying their burden. Leave their actions with them, turn 180 degrees and walk three to four feet away. Be fully in the present, without any chains tying you to the past.

Repeat the process with each person.

In leaving the perceived negative input with each person and walking away with gratitude for the lesson you learned, you will be open to a deeper level of healing within your heart and soul. Each person helped you to be strong enough to withstand the onslaught of life.

Welcome. You are on your way to becoming the master of your universe. You have within you your own pinnacle of power as an adult living in the now. You can be fully present with the lessons of the past behind you. With the burdens released you can walk forward into a more positive, stronger future. Yes, there will be challenges ahead. But now you realize what the purpose of challenges are, you can be fully present to face them head on with newfound strength.

7.

MANIFEST YOUR POSSIBILITIES

"Life is the vehicle that allows you to manifest the infinite possibilities of the Universe."

The Universe put in a special order for the conditions to be met for our existence. We received life from our parents and we were in agreement. We were born into a universe of possibilities that only we could fulfill. Now we can own that endowment and manifest those possibilities. Starting with gratitude towards ourself, our life and our parents.

After all the trouble we went through to incarnate, now is the time to recognize the gift of our existence. There is no time to waste. The credits will start rolling soon enough so the opportunity to create the next scene of the movie is now. Whatever we want this movie to be is up to us. Whether we create a masterpiece theater, a comedy or drama the choice is ours.

No matter what you choose, trust that the universe will support you. Your creation leads you to your fate and destiny. No matter what happens externally, you are in charge. Choose wisely because this is not a dress rehearsal. Allow yourself to expand and grow and mature into what you are destined to become.

We were born to achieve the highest good. If your life was

too easy, it would not be as meaningful when you had success. Life itself is Yin to Yang and Yang to Yin. It's a circle of sorts we all live in. It's time to catch up as the movie is playing. Whether it's Act 1, our formative years, Act 2, adulthood or the final curtain of Act 3. Consider these questions and write down the answers as you take on the roll of Director in your own life movie.

- What is in your script?
- What is the title?
- What has happened so far?
- Where is the plot going?
- Where do you want the plot to go?
- How will you change the plot to get there?
- Are you happy with the script?
- What can you change? How?
- How do you see yourself? Actor, Director, Writer?
- Where do you see yourself? Scenes? Locations?
- Who do you see yourself acting and or directing with?
- Who are your co-stars?
  Are you the co-star or the lead?
- What can you change?
- Would any changes give you more happiness?
- Would you rather stay out of the picture and
  let others play the parts?
- Is being the director more important than all else?
- What prevents you from directing, acting and
  starring in your own life movie?
- Describe the movie of your life?
- What changes in the script that need to be made?
- Which characters need new rolls, development,
  other changes?
- What will be the outcome with these changes?
- Do the changes make you happier?
- Do you feel empowered by these changes?

- Can you make the changes?
  If yes, how? If no, why not?
- Change the plot.
- Change the ending.

When the final credits roll, the cast of characters will show up at your funeral for the last scene. What would you like to hear them say?

"Poor soul. What a waste. At least he/she is at peace now."
Or
"Wow! That was a life lived on all levels. What an impact he/she had on me. Life will never be the same."

8.

LIFE IN THREE ACTS

ACT 1

Act 1 is the beginning of the story of our lives. Sometimes we were created "by accident" because our parents succumbed to the forces of nature which overtook them at their sexual union. Physical magnetism and orgiastic frenzy enmeshed them together. Whether we remember consciously or not, whatever occurs while we're in the womb contributes greatly to the script of our lives. While we wait in the wings unknowingly, at one with our mother, all her feelings and reactions to her forthcoming motherhood write their messages onto our mind, body, and soul.

When we made our debut, we were the star of the day. All eyes were upon us, hopefully welcoming us into the family if we were "wanted" or casting us asunder if we were not. Whatever the circumstances, we were a child star.

Our parents or other adults became directors during our formative years. They began impacting us from before the start. We learned through their behaviors, their attitudes and adapted their beliefs. This explains why our parents or other caregivers are the most influential people in our lives.

We live in the family home and are forced to live according to other people's rules. We adjust. We learn to cope with everyone else pulling the strings. It is all part of what we do before we grow into our own autonomy and find our very own place in our life. Weathering the storms of school, high school, and college are part of our formative years. Then we may gain the courage to call the shots and create what we want in Act 2. Whether we start a family, focus on career, travel, or a combination, everything we do is part of the mission and incarnation of what we came here to experience. Life has one goal — to move forward at all cost.

ACT 2

We survive the joy, trials, and tribulations of having other people direct our lives in Act 1. In Act 2 we take over the roles of director and creator as well as star. We may choose to get married and have children creating a *Father Knows Best* or *Leave It To Beaver* lifestyle. At some point it may turn into a *Divorce Court* melodrama. If our parents are aging a little *Terms Of Endearment* or *On Golden Pond* may crop up.

Act 2 is formative in a different way. We have been around the block a few times or more, gaining wisdom and courage so we can meet new challenges or opportunities that come our way. Life itself will always test us so that we can rise to the top or sink trying. It is our movie now and we have just *One Life to Live*.

If you choose a script that appeals to you, go the distance to get the ending you want. There is always room to change it along the way. Life is full of options. Be flexible and open to movements that may surprise you. A new cast of characters may show up to support or change you.

The other option is to be the star but let someone else be the director as we had in Act 1. We may then be victim of their whims and whimsies. We can give up control of the direction of our life even though your name is on the marquee. Yet this is rarely acceptable. Much better to jump in and make it our life.

Many people in our circle may feel threatened by our new-found independence and will try to take us down. Jealousy, fear, and betrayal run rampant in and outside of Hollywood. We must always stay on our toes.

It is now Act 2. There is no time to waste. We may be just a wrinkle away from an Eve Harrington emerging from Act 1 to take our place. But be careful not to fall into the trap of trying to stay youthful at the hands of the plastic surgeon.

This especially applies to women. By 40, even incredibly lovely women may be unjustly cast as grandma and no longer the romantic lead. Men, on the other hand, can sometimes extend Act 2 by remaining sexy and virile well into their 70's. Mick Jagger and Sean Connery have it covered as their Act 2 never seems to end. Women can and will have to write a new script to star in their own unique, self-created vehicle. *The Devil Wears Prada* but she can also be *Woman of the Year*.

ACT 3

We held our own in Acts 1 and 2. At this point many people may know what we've been through. We had the guts to stay relevant and survive.

Although we may still have time to write new scenes, much depends on the choices we've made throughout our lives. If we, at some point, cultivated our power of presence, we can enjoy Act 3 with serenity, ease, and a sense of accomplishment.

When it's over, a stone may rest on the ground marking our birth and death, a few words or phrases inscribed on it for posterity. Others in their Act 1 or 2 will take our place in the limelight. We pass the torch to them. Their Act 3 will come in time and the torch will be passed to another generation. As we exit stage left, the "Circle of Life" continues its never ending dance.

9.
THE GOAL
OF THIS BOOK

This goal of this book is to help you make sense out of the unseen forces in your life. These hidden energies guide you in many ways. They are the framework for what happens in your life. They are invisible yet subtle dynamics. One of the ways this hidden blueprint moves you along is by presenting challenges.

Facing life's challenges helps you learn. This makes you more flexible, resilient, and resourceful so are able to deal with unexpected changes as well as opportunities. Life is your teacher and friend even though, at times, it can seem like your enemy. Life teaches you through external stimuli to help you develop internally. The million dollar question is "What is your mission?"

- Where is your life going?
- What is its destination?
- What does it want to do with you on the journey?
- Is Life "Spirit" or is Spirit "Life?"

The goal of this book is simple. It is to introduce you to

the invisible aspects of your life. It is to explore the seemingly unconscious movements and share the lessons of your subtle internal dynamics that guide you in the world. The discoveries and insights are available to open your consciousness to the deeper realities that are unseen yet so influential in your life. It is these unseen forces that also influence how you react to situations and outside stimuli.

When you unlock what is hidden in your universe and your existence, you will learn about the secret force that resides in your subconscious or unconscious mind. When you have a new awareness, you will understand what is real. This will open a perspective for you that things are not what they may seem.

This book is to inspire your curiosity and enlighten your spirit with wisdom, understanding, and a little fun. The goal of *Master Your Universe* is to show you how the microcosm interfaces with the macrocosm on every level. Nature provides great insight into how instinct ensures survival. Whether you study the lives of insects, mammals, or human family systems, the hidden dynamics are there. You can explore life, death, family systems, your ancestors, as well as human history by observing earth.

Thank you for taking this journey. Hopefully it will help you make sense of your life and understand your unique place in the universe. We are often in reaction to the external world. Understanding that interaction will help you to see why you are responding to outside stimuli; which forces you inherited from your family and which reactions are genuinely yours.

PART TWO
LIGHTS!

10.
UNIVERSAL RULES OF ENGAGEMENT

The Universe operates on unconditional love. Life resonates with love. It is the pulse of creation, undulating, growing, seeking to know itself, striving for fulfillment on every level. Life takes joy expressing itself in the physical. Every dimension is included, seemingly both bad and good together simultaneously.

Life is an experiment. Things may be going one way then a twist is added to see how the participants will react. We agree to participate in the experiment because we are alive. Our human ego may kick and scream for things to be different, but our Soul knows its mission. Our Spirit signed up for the challenge to live and learn.

The Universe's mission is to learn and to grow. Growing means evolving. It is a priceless experience fraught with challenges which create resilience and strength to endure more life. In spite of any and all challenges, the Universe strives to move forward. Lessons are learned even if they are painful.

- The Universe loves life.

- The Universe loves love.

- The Universe embraces it all.

- The Universe seeks completion.

- The Universe loves to evolve.

- The Universe itself is a grand experiment.

- The Universe is the beginning and the end and everything in between.

- The Universe is you and you are the Universe.

11.

UNIVERSAL TRUTHS AND YOU

"There is no right, no wrong, just truth."

Truth is a matter of perception and, as we know, everyone has an opinion or deeply held belief as to what is right and what is wrong. Whoever thinks they are right seldom believes they are wrong. Most people never think that they are dishonest. Life goes on either way whether they have all the facts or not. Most people make decisions on the information that they have been given. With more awareness we can better understand whether we are conscious or not of the forces that guide the choices we are making.

To further complicate things, there are cultural, national, and even global belief systems existing in the present that can cloud our awareness. Always try to remember that history is written by the victors who minimize and marginalize the suffering, dramas, and traumas endured by the losing side and all of the collateral damage. Those who lost their lives and property have their stories to tell and deserve to be included in the history. Everyone is important. Everyone needs to be heard and accounted for.

It 'is the truth of all that will set us free. What is your truth? What remains hidden? What do you not see? Can you be conscious of your unconscious? If you knew more about your unconscious, would that affect your conscious? Would your choices be different?

What if your beliefs that you think are reality are not? Could a deeper truth be hidden in your soul or unconscious mind?

What if unseen realities you thought shaped your beliefs could be accessed to alter your perception? Would that allow you to make different choices?

Deep healing and changes in beliefs come from expanded consciousness. Many times healing happens when we let go of what we thought to be true. This expansion serves your body, mind, and soul in a profound way, making room for healing. Expanding your perception of reality allows you to experience the hidden multidimensional universal truth. Each realization can change your perception in a second, just as reading this sentence now becomes your past after you go on to the next word in front of you. We are continually moving towards the future in every nanosecond of our existence.

This truth creates new challenges to be fully present. The moment you just experienced is already in your past.

12.

TRANSCENDING FORGIVENESS

Today, many healers, seekers, and therapists have jumped on the dysfunctionality bandwagon without realizing the systemic consequences.

Bert Hellinger, renowned philosopher and developer of Constellation work and the Spirit-Mind Movements has reported for many years that there is a hidden symmetry and order to love.

As a facilitator of this modality, I find his bold statements to be true and will gladly help anyone explore and understand the philosophy and reasoning behind them. As always, let your heart decide what is right for you and your well-being.

One of Hellinger's more controversial theories is that practicing the "art of forgiveness" can be very damaging to the so-called "forgiver" on many levels. It may not serve their best interests no matter how well intentioned. The unintended consequence is that trying to practice "forgiveness" encourages a "superior" attitude that seeks to be "bigger than the perpetrator." This actually diminishes the release that conscious acceptance can bring about.

In this way the "forgiver' actually perpetuates the pain of

victimization in an unhealthful way — upon themselves and, unconsciously, upon others as well.

If the desired goal is to release oneself from pain and suffering in order to heal a deep wound and move beyond an endured atrocity, the very idea of "forgiveness" becomes detrimental to both the forgiver and the forgiven. Systemically speaking, we would call this being "too big," arrogant, or presumptuous because it removes responsibility from the perpetrator.

It also disrespects the bigger fate and destiny of our whole ancestral line. In doing so, the "forgiver" attempts to elevate him or herself to the "top" of the whole hierarchical system, as if he or she was the creator of life itself — showing pity on these poor little subjects under his or her command. In reality, the most recent addition to any larger family system has no right to judge those who came before, as they are the newer members in the larger hierarchical framework known as the family. This does not negate opinions and feelings, but if we truly want to break the cycle of perpetrator/victim, "forgiveness" is NOT the way to do it. Why? Because the victim carries both energies, thereby hurting themselves with a heavier load of toxic baggage that enslaves them to the past.

Re-SOUL-ution

There is a way out that is simple, profound, and completely healing, leading to a restoration of love, order and harmony for all concerned. This liberating state of "non-forgiveness" is "acceptance." We must be humble enough to acknowledge our place in the larger context of the multidimensional generation from whom we inherited our DNA. We received the gift of life through them as well as their suffering and turmoil. This dualistic condition can provide wonder and horror equally. The key is to honor and accept life itself as it is. This action of accepting imperfection (even the living dynamics of catastrophic change) will lead us back to inner and outer harmony, providing us with dignity and strength. These qualities will help us accept the gifts and challenges equally that life continually tosses in our path. It is the acceptance of everything "as it is" that will release us from the chains of the past and point you towards a better tomorrow. The humility of "acceptance" ironically empowers us. We did not create the cycle of life. We are merely a participant, and our day in the sun lasts for a very short time.

This is our chance to enjoy, transform and better ourselves, taking our rightful place in the family system. When we have honor and gratitude with acceptance, the cycle of inner slavery is broken. Our acceptance of life as it is, along with accepting our parents as they are, and our larger family system as it was, relieves us of our self-appointed role as judge and jury. To remain neutral without judgments also leads us to accept the good things we inherited more completely. By letting those who wronged or hurt us own their perpetrator/victim energy, we release ourselves from the entanglement and let the fate and responsibility rest where it belongs — with them.

This is not about blaming or shaming our family for the choices they made. It is about honoring our own part in it. The acknowledgement that comes with acceptance creates an energetic release. Incidents occurred in a place and time pre-dating our own creation and admission into the family system. Accepting these simple truths frees us and strengthens our resolve. There is no need to "forgive." Bow down in thankfulness and gratitude as you accept your life as the gift that it is.

13.

BOW DOWN

Poem by
Gary Stuart

Bow Down *to all those who came before, as they remain alive at your innermost core, seeing the world through your eyes.*

Bow Down *to the suffering and strife that your ancestors endured, surviving the conditions that led to your life.*

Bow Down *to all the pain that life may have caused, for you are the joy of their toil and labor that can't be ignored.*

Bow Down *yet again to your very own parents, even if their gifts to you were never apparent.*

Bow Down *to the mysteries of life that fail to make sense; it's God's way of showing there's always a chance.*

Bow Down *to it all, no matter what you think. If you do not stop to do this, your life could be gone in a blink.*

To **Bow Down** *is a humble act of honoring those who came before. If you can't Bow Down to your creator, then what in your life means more?*

Bow Down...

14.
THE POWER
OF ACCEPTANCE

As a child you were probably forced to accept the way you were treated by your family. Some situations were good as the adults took care of your well-being and others not so good. If there were any negative incidents by one parent, the other, or both, sometimes another relative can be our advocate, protector, or champion.

We may want our childhood or certain situations to be different than they were. We may waste so much time in "Shoulda, Coulda, Woulda" that we forget to be present in our life. Our lifetime is too short to waste on longing for a past that did not exist and really cannot be changed.

This can keep us trapped in a rut. Sometimes it seems we just can't escape from the fantasy story. A million things transpire between birth and adulthood. Why do we focus more on the negative events? It's funny how selective memory can be and how each person's ego can create an edited version of their movie that supports their most cherished beliefs, feelings, and story. Many try a myriad of therapies to sort things out in search of inner peace and resolution. Others continually react as if the negative events were still happening or create new ones that uncannily match events in the past.

The danger of trauma is that it creates or sets a pattern that becomes a "negative habit" or "comfort zone" well into adulthood. The original negative situation can be created over and over again very much like a caged hamster caught in a running wheel. For adults it is a self-made cage. We can feel like victims, unaware of the subtle ways we are perpetrating our own distress.

The real challenge is how to disengage from this self-destructive pattern or condition that does not serve you in a positive way. Becoming aware is a good place to start. Rather than think there is no problem and all, you can observe the cyclical pattern and your repeated reactions. Many people are unaware that their "comfort zone" is actually a loop of internal perpetrator/victim dynamics expressing themselves in the dramas of their lives. Those who are not conscious of their behavior are often quite happy being "self-righteously innocent," playing the victim against evil malicious, perpetrators who do them wrong. The long lasting impact of trauma lies in this "internalization of the aggressor." This internal aggressor actually becomes our own inner perpetrator aspect.

How do we engage or transform this? Can we transform our comfort zone? Can we regain our innocence?

When we understand the polarity of the perpetrator/victim dynamic, we may realize it is safe to release ourselves from the negative bond that was created in the past. Once we can admit these things, express these things, and feel these things in a new way the healing process can begin in earnest. As Bert Hellinger eloquently states, "we can only release after we embrace."

Can we honor the person, the place, and lesson this aspect of life created and put in our path? There is always a bigger reason why these events happen. Yes, we were wounded yet we survived. However, we can find the courage to release the negative hold and have acceptance for the place and the lesson it brought to our life.

We were strong enough as children to survive the trauma and reached adulthood in spite of it. We have the strength to embrace the situation by facing it. Let the past be the past, be fully present in the now. We may have scars but the wounds can finally heal. Our perception and behaviors may change as well. After we honor our fate and destiny by accepting this "perpetrator element," we can find freedom to leave the past in the past and put it to rest with a clear future in front of us. In a sense, our innocence can be restored.

15.

THE HIDDEN POWER OF THE VICTIM VS THE HIDDEN WEAKNESS OF THE PERPETRATOR

Most see victims as weak who are preyed on by perpetrators of all sorts. With the focus on the victim's suffering it is easy to overlook the hidden strength of the victim. Victims are strong even if they were children at the time of the survived offense. Most sexually abused children make it to adulthood and become parents themselves in spite of negative experiences from a relative or stranger during their formative years. Some may carry the trauma forward. Others could have stunted growth, health issues, or mental problems. Despite their current issues, they were strong enough to survive and thrive. They have a hidden strength in them that is actually more powerful than their perpetrator.

The perpetrator is weak. They seek their false power through a child or younger, smaller person. The victim is the stronger of the two. Any perpetrator may have the strength to overpower their victim mentally, physically, or sexually. Even though the perpetrator was usually a victim first, this rationale does not let them off the hook. They are still responsible for their actions. Could they be reacting to the powerlessness they felt when they too were victimized in their youth? Could that false sense of power cover-up the helplessness they experienced? Could they be trying to compensate to find the strength they lost? Could they be pushing away their own toxic feelings acquired when they were abused? Maybe they became part of the perpetrator cycle to transform the bad feelings they had as a victim.

The purpose of this book is to empower you to look at the subconscious aspects of your soul and intuitive intellect. Every person has an Internal Aggressor and Outer Victim. Everyone has perpetrator and victim dynamics within themselves and their lives.

You have sunny days with beautiful weather then stormy days with wind, rain, hail, and lightening. Think of the bad weather as perpetrator/aggressor energy you must be subservient to as the forces it contains are bigger than you. You can easily become victim to uncontrollable storms, winds, and rains. You contain both polarities; the power to perpetrate, which may manifest quietly or subtly, and the same capability to be a victim, working against yourself or others. They are both sides of the same coin, no better and no worse. You can vacillate between the two extremes in subtle ways. It can be as simple as wanting to diet and then eating chocolate cake with a Diet Coke. Another example — not quitting smoking when you know you need to. Each time you break your own rule, you perpetrate against yourself. Every time you smoke, it is one step closer to death. If these simple acts don't show you how your inner perpetrator/outer victim energy works, nothing will.

Your mind can play tricks on you to make you think you are not hurting yourself when indeed you are. Self-sabotage is the best term to describe this pervasive dynamic which everyone embodies at one time or another. Both of these dynamics perpetuate change. It embodies both Creation and Destruction. The wheel turns using opposing energies. We inhabit this wheel not of our own creation and are at the effect of all who partake in this life. There is no choice other than to participate. The alternative to not participate is commonly known as death.

Look at your birth. It was the destruction of your fetal existence within your mother's womb. You had to break through into a new reality. This reality seems to enjoy building tenacity, resilience, and strength.

Let your work begin. Be honest with yourself. Answer the following questions:

1. What is not working in your life?

2. Why can't you change what is not working?

3. What stops you?

4. Why do you let things stop you?

5. Do you see yourself as a victim?

6. What do you gain from suffering?

7. Are you happy being stuck with your destructive habits?

Can you take an honest look at yourself and admit that you create the causes for this to happen? If it is external elements, list 5 things out of your control.

What or who empowers you to create the life you want to live?

List 5 things you do to change your life and let the Universe support you in a new way.

In what ways can you mitigate your fear of change?

List 5 things that excite you.

List 5 things on what your life would look like if you lived it with more awareness.

There's only one thing left to do. Go out and create it. What are you waiting for? Your time is now. Repeating what does not work is insanity. The universe will support you, as it supports of all creation. You deserve to live an empowered life.

16.

POP CULTURE VS THE POWER OF PRESENCE

L ife is full of possibilities. And when we're in touch with where we want our life's journey to take us, we find that the choices we make can help move us in the right direction.

However, life is also full of distractions. A little *Pulp Fiction* can be a fun diversion now and then, but since pop culture tends to transport us to the most superficial of realms, a little can go a very long way. It also emphasizes the external, which hardly encourages introspection. Some people tend to make excuses and blame external forces for anything negative in their life. And you don't have to be a "Real Housewife of..." wherever to fall into the trap. But every time we do this, we are defining ourselves as a victim.

This is why it is so important for us to realize we have a choice. And that choice comes from recognizing the power of the present moment. It's what I like to call the "Power of Presence." It's what makes your life P.O.P. The most personal power we have is that of choice, and it can take us so much deeper than pop culture ever allows us to go.

I have included certain exercises in this book to help you

create new thought forms and new ways of viewing yourself in the world. So often we tend to use the challenges in our lives as something to rally against, as if life itself was our enemy. Life can be what you want it to be, and if you want it to be an enemy, it will be. Those challenges, rather, can be opportunities for you to cultivate your resilience and strength. Just ask any weed growing in a crack in an asphalt parking lot.

No matter what you may think, we bring on some of these challenges ourselves. In other words, we are not as innocent as we might think. There are many levels of entanglement, and even some comfort in being a victim. But when we stand in our own power of presence, we start to shed those subtle layers of victimhood that keep us from feeling fully in control of our lives. It really is about recognizing that you have a choice. What you choose to do and believe affects you at every minute of every day. You might just as well focus on what serves you and moves you forward. Regardless, there is something to be learned. The question is, do you want to learn by being a victim or from being in a position of strength?

It is time to use what you know to change your perception of what you don't know. Then there will be space for something new to come into your life, your heart, and your soul. Many people deny that they engage in self-sabotaging behavior. But once we acknowledge that we do, we can begin to develop a different strategy, allowing us to react in a more positive and fulfilling way. Once we embrace the fact that sometimes we are our own worst enemy, then we are free to change our pattern of behavior and move in a different direction.

The ultimate goal is E-M-P-O-W-E-R-M-E-N-T!

You do not need to find a director, as you already have the job. And you are also the star. Once you recognize the power of the present moment, you can shape the story of your life however you wish. There are many behind-the-scenes dramas that may distract you from time to time. Your family is #1. But the *Catch22* is that you would not be here without them.

Every feature film and its cast of characters has a backstory. And as we see in film, and in real-life Constellation workshops, the current action is impacted by the dynamics of that backstory. When we see someone else's story up on the big screen, it's easy to see how their past may be holding them back and keeping them from reaching their goals. In our own lives, however, the correlation may not be so obvious. That's where this modality can prove invaluable. It can allow you to witness your own story from a more objective point of view, like a member of an audience. From this perspective, it becomes more clear what is needed in order to break with certain patterns, including patterns of thought, that may be holding you back.

Now any director worth his salt knows how to change the tone, meaning, or context of any scene within the film he's creating. Therefore, no matter how the script was initially written, we have the power to change what happens within each scene as it takes place. This is what I mean when I speak of the "Power of Presence." We can rewrite, recast, re-edit, and redirect our lives at any time. But whenever it takes place, it happens in the now. Even our reactions to and perceptions of things in the past can be altered in the present. And a good way to start is to consider that the things you thought were holding you back can actually be used to support you. In other words, it's not about freeing yourself from your past, it's about freeing yourself from your old perceptions of your past.

As the lead character, you have studied and lived with this story your whole life. The story line is familiar, as is the backstory. Understanding this as well as the invisible effects on the other characters is invaluable in making any changes you may desire. It's your narrative. It should please you no matter what any other audience member may think. You are the one who has to be satisfied, as this movie is your life and no one else's. You're not just a co-star or extra in someone else's story. You have a story of your own. Don't be afraid to tell it.

Living in the now is a very powerful place to be. As long as you are alive, you harness your own "Power of Presence." In other words, you have the amazing ability to make your life "P.O.P." Now it's time to enjoy it!

17.

ODE TO THE POSITIVE

Hidden underneath the external negatives and beliefs lies a quiet positive force seeking to break through into a new reality. Honor the perceived negative to gain access to the underlying positive that actually contains our power.

What is this power? It is the power to create our own reality in any way we see fit. Victims love to commiserate with other victims so they never feel alone. As the saying goes misery loves company.

However, the positively empowered seek fulfillment in the now. The positive movement is to fulfillment and fruition to make any and all dreams come true.

Inspire others to be positive. Bathe in Unconditional Love. Love beyond duality. Wholeness is embracing all aspects simultaneously!

18.

UNCONDITIONAL LOVE

Poem by
Gary Stuart

Loving the dark as well as the light is challenging to most who judge and fight. They assume that they are most always right, not understanding humanities plight.

All darkness exists to add balance to light. It gives us a glimpse during each night, as without so called darkness we wouldn't know light.

Light itself exists to shine on all things. It brings clarity to darkness and shines on its wings. Both take delight watching each other take flight.

One day all people will stop fighting to see that darkness resides in you as it does inside me.

There is no other apart from within thee as loving both equally helps all agree to love. Life in its wholeness helps us to see that darkness brings light for all hearts to be.

That's true unconditional love as you too soon may see.

PART THREE

CAMERA!
REWRITE
THE
WRONGS

.

19.

WHAT ARE YOU WAITING FOR?

We are the dreams come true of those who came before. Is time really on your side? It is and it isn't. As John Lennon stated so eloquently "Life is what happens while you're making other plans." You may think that you have all of the time in the world. You are born with an expiration date. You live day to day. The days turn into weeks; the weeks turn into months which turn into months and years. If you are lucky you evolve and enjoy the time. Life is the gift that was given to you by those who came before.

If you cannot dream it, how can it happen?

Do not hesitate or wait for the dream to manifest because time passes fast.

There is no time to waste.

Realizing your dream takes work, dedication, and responsibility. You have the power to create the causes to manifest your dream. The Universe is waiting to support you in any way possible. You have the power to harness creation through intention and manifest whatever you want. The *Catch-22* is the Universe knows it has Eternal Time and you do and do not. Many believe we "sow the seeds" in one lifetime for the next." Take possession of your life now. Your destiny and fate depend on it. You have the opportunity to go with or against your own flow.

As we said before, as long as you are alive you have your own "Point of Presence." Remember you have the ability to make your life "P.O.P." Living in the now is a very powerful place to be. Many do not know how much power they possess. It can be used in negative or positive ways. Both bear their own intended and unintended lessons and consequences.

You are endowed with your own personal power to go with the flow and even create the flow in any direction you would like. You have the power to "P.O.P." any way you choose. Life does not discriminate either way. It has its own flow. You can also be a "victim" of life and its flow as well. I will let you in on a big secret: Life does not care.

Its only goal is to move forward at all cost and it does not ever look back.

20.

THE MEANING OF LIFE: THE BIG PICTURE

Surprisingly, many people actually choose to be a "Victim of Life." They become comfortable in the role of blaming others for their situation without realizing they are "secret perpetrators" in their own right.

Victims can unconsciously hinder their own movement forward by being mired in the self-righteous glory of being better. The same goes for the delusions of the perpetrator. They are flip sides of the same coin. The cruel irony is that both perpetrators and victims feel they are on the moral high ground and do not claim responsibility for their choices. Victims often think they look noble compared to perpetrators. Both wear badges of honor: Perpetrators for perceived strength and victims for tenacity.

A victim may start to identify so strongly with that title that he or she may begin to embrace it with almost fanatical fervor. It is important not to keep victimizing yourself by continuing to define who you are in those terms. Doing so may be keeping you stuck in a reaction to a time and circumstance that no longer exists, and not allowing you to be fully present in your life here and now. Sometimes we also may carry the "victim energy" for someone in our family line. If they suffered, we'll suffer. But this is actually not the best way to honor their memory. Let their story be just that — their story. Taking on their baggage doesn't lighten their load, and only bogs us down with things that aren't ours to carry.

We see this play out in Constellation work all the time. A perpetrator can be a victim, and a victim can be a perpetrator. To avoid becoming entangled with the energy of either, we need to find a sense of compassion for both. There really is no separation of consciousness. We are all one sharing a universal experience. There is no good. There is no bad. There are just lessons to be learned. And remember, every perpetrator was most likely a victim first. This does not excuse such behavior, but it can provide insight into its origin.

Again, the point is to not let any victimization define you, or cause you to become stuck in a pattern of fear and mistrust. Actually, it's not that fear, in and of itself, is bad. Fear can be a necessary life-saving device built into our nervous system for survival. The goal, however, is to not to let it stop you from making the jump into the life you deserve. Do you want "Shoulda, Coulda, Woulda" on your tombstone?

And even when you manifest your dreams, they still come with a fear of the unknown. Those same neurons that produce fear reactions in our minds and bodies can also be perceived as excitement and adventure. There is a balance to both. Perhaps make a list of positive and negative outcomes from what you perceive your choices to be, and let life do the rest.

The Universe will support you if you let it.

But can you trust it to do so? This is the $64,000 question. I say choose excitement, then fasten your seat belt for the ride of your life. Be aware that worry, procrastination, hesitation, and fear may still be lurking in the background, behind the scenes, never too far away. But opportunity may not wait or put up with indecision or trepidation.

Life is your gift to do with as you please. Everything is

gained and nothing is lost. In the spiritual realm, it is about personal evolution and learning on a soul level. The goal is to master your universe.

If this seems problematic for you, don't worry. You're not alone, You can still make this your "Point of Presence" to create the destiny and future that you want. Life may have other plans, but you have the chance to demonstrate your true character on many levels. Be mindful, generous, and humble with the gifts you have been given, and remember to give in return.

Build bridges of appreciation; help those in need; support, support, support. Let the universe be as friendly to you as you are to the universe. The internal or external universe represents unlimited creativity and expansion in all directions simultaneously. Do the same and see what appears. Sharing your inner gifts sends a message out to the universe of potential. Pay the gift you have received forward. At the very least you are in line with life. Life flows and expands for eternity so it will come back either now or later as good fortune. Paying it forward lends itself to love. Only good can come from spreading love into the eternal spectrum of universal possibility. Unless, of course, you always find yourself rooting for the serial killer, but that's another story with its own set of plot twists.

Let yourself enjoy the prosperity you have already been gifted. When we come from a place of gratitude rather than entitlement, we allow ourselves to be open to receive even more. And I'm not just talking tangibles here. Every Citizen Kane eventually realizes that the simplest "rosebud" can mean more than all the acquired wealth in the world. The trick is to learn the lesson before it's too late to apply it. Even if you're cash poor, you can still amass a large amount of positive karma in your spiritual bank account.

Realize that while money is handy,
it never buys you happiness.

Support and accept others as they are.

Don't be afraid to share.

Discover and own your Power of Presence.

Stay the course and be courageous.

Remain humble.

Arrogance and narcissism can be very sneaky. And even if you are successful, watch out for the yes men and sycophants who may prop you up for their own gain, only to tear you down behind your back. Jealously is poison and many people have two faces. Trust your gut. It is seldom wrong. You can still live and love while watching and observing with wisdom and compassion.

Your destiny and fate are in your own hands. Life and the Universe may have other plans. Being proactive and taking charge of as much as you can is the goal. The ultimate destination may be unknown, but don't let that stop you. Let it inspire you. The journey of a lifetime is ours to enjoy. Whether or not we do is up to us.

The universe supports those who dare.

Ask Columbus.

Ask Einstein.

Ask Jonas Salk.

Ask Martin Luther King Jr.

Ask Gandhi.

Ask Hitler. This is the biggest irony of all.

The universe supports all equally: The good, the bad and the ugly. In the bigger picture, there is something to learn from all of it.

PART FOUR
ACTION!

21.

FINDING YOUR FOCUS

We enter into this world positive, happy, and giggly. We enjoy play, getting nurtured, and having fun making new discoveries. But as we grow into adulthood, we often forget our natural state of play, joy, and wonder. Life itself often hardens and distracts us from the way we were when the curtain first went up. We take the cues from our family system regarding what it takes to belong, even though such conformity often means betraying or losing touch with our true self.

We need to remember what a great pleasure it is to be alive. Your soul has a mission. Your life has a purpose. And we can get back to that realization at any time. You can start over at any moment. You can begin living your life in a new way at any point. You can be that happy baby again, regardless of how many wrinkles are now on that baby face.

The key lies in letting go of the patterns of behavior and/or belief that have not been serving you. You can once again feel that sense of newborn wonder, even if you're in your *On Golden Pond* years. It's never too late to rediscover happiness, experience joy, allow yourself have a laugh, and get back to living the life that was your birthright all along.

Even if we've been letting others write the script for us for years and years, we can begin a rewrite at any time. Don't give final script approval to anyone else.

One good way to help yourself get back in touch with your own needs is to set some short-term and attainable goals. In the movies, as in real-life, goals help elicit action. A goal, however, cannot be met without also setting a positive intention.

Ask yourself:

- What inspires you?

- What propels you to act?

- What fulfills you the most?

- What makes your heart sing?

- What makes you smile?

- Why not live with an intention of inspiration?

- Why waste your time?

By living an inspired life, you can make your dreams a reality and make your heart sing with delight. The universe will support you and help you live your life on purpose as opposed to by accident. Inspiration is contagious. Take the lead at home, at work, with family and friends. *It's a Wonderful Life*, and when we live it with integrity and joy, we inspire others to do the same.

If you are not sure what inspires you, make this the year you find out. Uplift and empower yourself. The same energy it takes to keep yourself down can be redirected to lift you up to wondrous new heights. It is all a matter of perception and framing.

There can be so much more in store for you. Take a chance,

open the door to being positive, and harness the goodness you deserve. The start of something new is the perfect chance to change. Write a new story, one in which you succeed on every level, have everything you want, and reach every goal.

Inspiration is the cure from the disease of procrastination. Now is the time to step it up. It is your life and your time to take charge of it. If you don't make your dreams come true, who will?

Trust and have faith in yourself, and the rest will follow. Ask your friends what about you inspires them. If they say nothing, get new friends.

22.

THE TIME OF YOUR LIFE!

Poem by
Gary Stuart

This is the time. It's the time of your life!
Does it inspire you or mire you in strife?

It's the time of your life! Are you standing with pride?
Do challenges please you or freeze you inside?

It's the time of your life! Are you using it well?
Do you live life or fear it? Your spirit can tell.

It's the time of your life! Do you reap its reward?
Do your blessings get counted or mounted and stored?

It's the time of your life! Are your passions ablaze?
Or are you just passing/amassing the days?

It's the time of your life! Are your banners unfurled?
Are you feeling enthused by or used by the world?

It's the time of your life! Are you living your truth?
Can that fire be rekindled that's dwindled since youth?

It's the time of your life! It's right now. It's today.
Don't let it be squandered and pondered away.

It's the time of your life! But the time may not last.
You may find while you worried it hurried on past.

It's the time of your life! It's the life that you've got.
It's time to start living it – ready or not!

·

23.
REDISCOVERING HAPPINESS

Every life has its trials and tribulations. We get angry; we get sad. We get depressed; we get frustrated. But this is also where we get a choice. We may not be able to eliminate problems from our lives, but we can choose how we react to them.

So often, we tend to fall into "reaction mode" before we're able to really get in touch with what we're feeling. When we can stop and consider what we're actually reacting to, we have the opportunity to make a different choice. And yes, happiness is a choice.

We don't need to eradicate the problems and stresses from our lives in order to be happy, but we can learn how to transform them. The Constellation work I've mentioned can help reveal the underlying issues to which we've been reacting, allowing a different reaction to be possible. People acquire all sorts of habits; frustration and anger can definitely become a pattern of behavior — a "go to" reaction, if you will. Patterns can be broken, and habits can be changed but sometimes we need a change of perspective.

If there's one thing I see over and over again, it's how much we're willing to carry for our families. We take on all sorts of burdens and baggage that we really don't have to, yet we do so out of love, and to feel we belong. Even a feeling of estrangement can be a way of belonging. But when we are able to recognize what is someone else's issue that perhaps we've taken on, we begin to develop the strength to disentangle ourselves from their sadness, distrust or anger. Allowing them to carry their own stuff, so to speak, helps to free us from any learned reactions and re-establishes a sense of individuality.

As newborns, we had not yet begun to take on the weights of the world. Healthy babies radiate joy, love, and happiness. They only cry to get their bodily needs met. They're positive, hopeful, and playful, living in and appreciating each present moment. As adults, we still have the same capacity. In other words, it is possible to get back to your natural, happy, joyful self.

No matter how many deep, dark secrets may lie in the shadows of your family tree, you can still emerge into the light. Even those who may have had a horrible atrocity befall them when they were a child can still regain that sense of inner peace that was forced from them so many years ago. It's not about becoming innocent again, it's about re-connecting with those feelings which innocence afforded.

You are strong. No matter what difficulties you may have gone through, you were strong enough to endure the original traumatic event, and you are strong enough to let it go. Don't let the familiarity of the trauma or pain stop you from releasing it. Good will take its place. But you have to be willing to let it.

The following is a great exercise to help you understand where you are at this point in your life, and what you can do in order to move forward. Give it a try. The more energy you invest, the more benefit you will receive.

Write Your Own Obituary Exercise:

You have a lot of things you want to accomplish in your life. But for right now, fast-forward to the end of your life. Write your own obituary. Describe what you want it to say about your accomplishments. Once you have completed it, answer the following questions:

1. Have you accomplished everything you described in your obituary?

2. What have you not accomplished yet?

3. Are you happy?

If there are things you still want to do, disentangling yourself from your old patterns of behavior or belief could be a great place to start. Whatever is blocking your ability to reach your potential can be discovered and cleared out of your way. The field of consciousness we access in Constellation work can show you what's been keeping you from reaching your goals and realizing your dreams.

A Constellation process can show you where you need to learn and grow. It can also show you where your ancestors got stuck in their lives. This may be a mirror of where you're getting stuck now. Once that energy is cleared, you'll find it much easier to move forward in your life now, because you'll no longer feel a loyalty to their limitations or lack of fulfillment.

When we free ourselves from the familial dramas passed down from previous generations, we are able to rediscover and reclaim the inherent happiness we felt when we first entered this world. But it's also important to remember that happiness isn't something that we eventually find further down the "Yellow Brick Road." If we think of happiness as something in the future, by that definition we'll never have it. We need to be appreciative for what we have right here, right now. The adage about having an "attitude of gratitude" could not be truer.

And, funny thing, when we're truly appreciative of even the smallest things we have, we allow ourselves to be open to receiving even more. Conversely, when we concentrate on what we don't have, we block ourselves from having the appreciation we need for more to come our way.

Sure, we inherited a certain amount of dysfunction from our family system, but they also gave us the gift of life. And that's no insignificant gift. It's everything. And it's something to be grateful for.

Life may continue to challenge us, but we can meet those challenges with a sense of gratitude for the opportunity to overcome them. And as every good tin man knows, that gratitude is at the heart of our ability to find the joy in every step of our journey.

24.

APPRECIATE LIFE: GRATITUDE IN THE PRESENT

In reality we often have an over abundance of choices. If we can put our egos down and let our heart open to what we did receive rather than what we did not, we will often be quite surprised to see new opportunities right in front of us that we didn't even realize were there. It seems quite futile to try and hold onto a past that did not happen the way we wanted it too. Sadly, this is a waste of time. Life really is a precious present every moment. That's why it's so important to learn from the past, let it go, and create the new life we want now. Our goal is to reveal and heal the hidden dynamics that may be sabotaging us in our lives.

When we accept life as it is, we can move forward with the strength, wisdom, and grace life's experiences provided. We can feel gratitude for what we've received. We can accept the way things were and leave what does not serve us behind. We do not have to be tormented by recriminations over what did or did not happen. Sometimes we may need to grieve for what we thought we wanted and needed but didn't get. Then we can open up to the realization that life itself is the greatest gift that could ever have been bestowed upon us.

25.

LIFE:
A BALANCING ACT

Babies are usually born fairly happy but then they absorb negative things they have trouble understanding, especially since they don't have the language to communicate what they see, hear, and feel. As they share joy and happiness with their parents, all too often there are more than just good feelings to understand. Babies are often incredibly in-tune with their parents even though they don't have the capacity to understand "Adult Stuff." They pick up on the subtle energies of the family field in deeply profound ways and are born with an innate desire to serve the family in some way.

The mere act of birth alters the whole family system. The couple become parents, their parents become grandparents, and the grandparents become great grandparents. The sweet, innocent newborn creates an instant shift in the family dynamics as its newest member. Thus, the role of every person in the family shifts in an instant. Each new baby moves life forward, giving hope for a better day and renewal for all those that came before.

As they say "We all come from a long line of dead people" Life, renewing itself constantly, flows amidst the generations.

As numerous babies are born, many other beings are leaving the system. We can see how birth, life, and death balance out in a circular way.

Standing up in life takes courage and strength. There are many challenges and experiences that will test us to our core and reveal both sorrow and joy. Life seems to enjoy roughing us up so we can be tough and resilient. Unfortunately babies sometimes have to bear so much more than adults because they cannot fight back.

Constellations can reveal unresolved grief that has lasted for centuries. The grief may also tragically show up as disease in subsequent generations. Ironically, it can feel like an unconscious badge of courage to honor someone who suffered greatly by carrying on their suffering; thereby not letting them be forgotten. The more unresolved events in the past, the more problems there can be down the line. Constellations allow you to go up-line and resolve the dynamics from before. Essentially you are clearing negative energy and entanglements for the past in the present day. Ancient dynamics hang around until every member of any family system is included.

Constellations teach us not to ignore the dead. We can honor them, acknowledge them, and appreciate them. We don't have to recreate the same situation they had. We don't have to finish their lives for them either. Instead, when we acknowledge their suffering with respect, we can leave their pain with them and move forward in our own lives free of their burdens.

Instead of carrying their unconscious negative energy, we honor our ancestors and ourselves best by staying alive, healthy, and making the most of our time in the spotlight. Constellations offer us a way to transform any negative dramas that we unconsciously inherited into consciously artistic, creative productions. They give us the power to transform and release anything is not ours to carry. We can leave the past on the cutting room floor, stand proudly in the present, move forward with strength.

The weather is a great metaphor for life. Nature uses violent activity to create change and renewal through wind, hurricanes, tornados, storms, floods, avalanches, volcanoes, and the like. If no people are injured, it is a non-issue. Once human life is threatened, it is a "disaster." If we did not have these violent storms or tornadoes, we would not have a beautiful planet full of diversity and ecosystems. Earth herself became a beautiful goddess by being pummeled by asteroids and attacked in space. The result is a garden paradise.

PBS and NOVA released an excellent special titled *Our Strange Days On Planet Earth*. It was about changes going on throughout the planet. The episode on Yellowstone National Park was fascinating. It was about our human beliefs about violence perpetrators, predators, and victims.

Scientists noticed through a chance photograph of a river in Yellowstone National Park that the ecosystem has changed drastically in the past seventy years. They examined aspen tree core samples in an attempt to see why the trees stopped growing.

What they found next was that in the 1930's 100,000 wolves were killed, ostensibly to protect the tourists visiting the National Park. Within 3-4 generations the willow trees disappeared from the river banks, the aspens stopped growing, beavers, birds, and other aquatic life disappeared. This did not happen outside of Yellowstone, only inside the national park. Scientists were baffled.

What does one predator have to do with all of this passive destruction? How could the top of the food chain affect everything below it? How could the lack of a predator destroy the forest, the trees, the vegetation, and all the animals? It did.

After the wolves were killed, deer overproduced from lack of a predator. The deer foraged without inhibition and destroyed the willows and new sprigs of aspen trees until they depleted the trees. The beavers were left with nothing. The ecosystem changed without the top predator to keep everything in balance.

Armed with this information, 100 wolves were reintroduced into the Yellowstone Valley. Immediately the wolves began killing the deer. Amazingly, the willow and aspen trees began growing back among the bones of the deer carcasses. Beavers came back to the river. Ecological balance and harmony was restored.

As a Hellinger-Certified Constellation Facilitator, I am awestruck by the similarity in perpetrator/victim dynamics that we work with during the Constellation process. Is there an ecosystem of the Soul? Does mankind operate within the same paradigm as the wildlife in Yellowstone Valley? Are predatory perpetrators essential to the health of our species? Is overpopulation acting like an aggressive perpetrator destroying life-giving environments?

There seems to be an inherent harmony in the divine balance. It seems more destruction ensues by trying to control and manipulate the unseen balance. Mankind thinks he knows but yet barely comprehends the wondrous complexity of life.

Keep in mind that there are predatory forces everywhere and they frequently appear as dynamics in Constellations. Believe it or not every family system contains these seemingly unconscious dynamics which is in part a microcosm of the world at large. Historically there are obvious predators, from Attila the Hun to Caesar, Stalin, and Hitler. As in nature, where wolves balance the ecosystem, predators seem to be necessary for balance and growth. If we can objectively step back and look with clarity maybe we'll see that wars and revolutions serve a higher good unseen amid the turmoil and trauma. Overpopulation and starvation may actually be balancing agents in the greater ecosystem of the Soul. It is as if life itself needs resistance and challenges to strengthen its resolve so it can move forward unencumbered by beliefs and judgements of what is "good" or "bad."

26.

TRANSFORMING THE PERPETRATOR/VICTIM CYCLE

The hardest dynamic to heal is one of the Perpetrator and Victim. The wounds created are deep, hidden and frequently get passed from generation to generation. Each person chooses which one to be and sometimes plays both. No matter which role you are in at the moment, you will see the worst of life through either of those perspectives. But however bad it is, you are still alive and functioning so know that on a soul level it is working. You CAN escape and be a healthy adult by making better choices. Freedom may scare you but when you experience how alive and joyful you feel, it will make all the struggle worth it. The alternative is endlessly repeating a negative pattern that does not serve you.

In a Constellation Healing experience we deal with both ancestral and current life dynamics of perpetrator/victim energy. Constellations give us a way out, a way to regain our lost innocence by freeing us from destructive negative entanglements. Although it seems true that life itself does not care either way, it can also be true that what doesn't kill us can make us more resilient, stronger, smarter, and more conscious of what life itself has to offer.

The biggest irony in perpetrator/victim dynamics is that no one ever lets go of it. What does more damage — the actual event or not being able to let it go be over it? Allowing the event to be in the past and not affect the present equals healing. What if the real issue that creates the trauma over and over again in our lives emanates from the subtle dynamic of the victim feeling superior to a perpetrator?

Does forgiveness free the victim or enslave them to the perpetrator? Do we choose to keep the entanglement going thus becoming our own perpetrator or double victim? Can we ever recover if we think we are superior to those who did us harm?

The key to understanding can be discovered within your family system through a Constellation Healing Experience. In Constellation work we can say what has never been said, experience the whole family drama from multiple points of view, thereby gaining the wisdom that comes from sitting in the audience for a little while and viewing the interactions of your family on the stage. Now, as an observer, rather than a participant, you can finally see what has been actually going on around you while you were acting out just your part. It's like waking up from a dream. You can get relief, a kind of "Ah-ha" moment where you finally get why things happened the way they did. Often compassion and sympathy for both the family "Victims" and "Perpetrators" wells up spontaneously and all can be accepted as it was.

Then you can honor your experience with your family and give respect for the lessons learned even, and especially when, the lessons were painful. You can bow with compassion to the people and events in your family that previously made you hurt, angry, and afraid. You can leave the perpetrator energy in the past with all it's accompanying hurt, guilt, shame, pain, and anger. Once you see it, you can turn and walk away, leaving it in the past.

It's somehow helpful to remember that most perpetrators

were victims first. They may recreate the trauma to ease their own pain and reenact the event to get release. Maybe they do it to get relief from guilt and the very act transfers their feelings. They are ashamed and angry about being a victim themselves that by feel better by becoming the opposite. This is the commonly known phenomenon called the "cycle of abuse." They want to transfer the burden of shame, pain, and guilt they experienced to someone who was as innocent as they were when it happened to them. Bert Hellinger once stated, "To be alive is to be guilty."

Hellinger also said, "Children blame. Adults take responsibility." Let's not let unfortunate events stunt our growth so that we never emotionally grow up. We need to face the inconvenient truths life has brought upon us. Where there is emotional addiction or codependency within the perpetrator/ victim relationship, it can often be healed through Constellation work.

Like Dorothy in *The Wizard of Oz*, you have always had the power, you just forgot how to use it. With awareness, you can take charge and move forward beyond those moments of life where you experienced a loss of power.

Once you see, accept, and release yourself from your entanglements with your ancestor's pain and tragedy, it can stay in the past and you can use the strength, fortitude, and resilience they did have to propel you through life smoothly like a steady wind in your sail. The goal is to find and restore what Hellinger called the "Order of Love" in your family.

The "Orders of Love" is the hidden sense of belonging which presents itself as a hierarchy in family systems (and even business organizations.) The rule is everyone has an equal right to belong but there is a hierarchy in terms of birth order, those born first are ranked highest, while subsequent members are lower. Parents are there to give and children to receive.

The integrity of the system may be violated in many ways. People, including young children, die through accidents, illness, disease, and are not mourned, previous partners in relationships are denied and hidden, experiences during war are not remembered or discussed, and many other types of family secrets remain in the background acting like energetic ghosts which can haunt subsequent generations. The effects come out in negative ways such as suicide, depression, mental or physical illness, addictions, lethargy, usually without any conscious awareness of what has happened in previous generations. Children grow up entangled with their parents, either inappropriately involved in their business or rejecting them entirely, hoping to make them feel better by taking on the suffering themselves.

Many of us judge our parent's actions but it is not our true place to do so. We will never know how or why our parents made the choices they made. They were playing a part themselves, acting unconsciously in line with the Grandparent's choices as well. When we judge them with a quasi-superior attitude we go against this natural order. It prevents us from really loving them in their totality and, more importantly, deeply receiving the gift of life we were given. To honor and respect what came before, we observe and accept the "good" and the "bad" as it was. This observing utilizing our "" allows us to finally appreciate the good as we move forward, leaving the bad in the past with them. This creates a healthy boundary between past and present.

The "Order of Love" applies not just to parents and ancestors but also to sibling birth order. An older child may unconsciously choose to be a perpetrator or victim within the confines of the family on behalf of the siblings. For example, an older child unconsciously "chooses" to take on abuse in order to protect the younger members. The other siblings may react or comply with an opposite behavior. Dysfunctional dynamics and behaviors take the place of functional, healthy bonds. You could call it a "familial comfort zone." It is a way of being part of a family that suits the personalities and cements your place within the order.

Negative behaviors or problem children receive a secondary gain from their siblings and parents. There may have been an ancestor from a previous generation who did the same exact replication from yet another place and time before. It is like there is a spiritual link or an invisible blueprint that is followed by everyone.

Loyalty and connection whether it is functional or dysfunctional is prevalent in all families. Life's inherent goal is to move forward at all cost. Siblings can also be invisibly connected to missing and dead ancestors too. Either way everyone belongs and has their rightful place. Everyone may be fighting for position and place within the system reacting to the invisible dynamics they did not create.

27.
THE BACKSTORY

Loyalty may be the single and biggest force that invisibly ties everyone to their family system. This is true even if your family is dysfunctional. There is comfort and familiarity in what is known. The flip side of loyalty is betrayal. Think of something as simple as the holidays. When a couple has to make a decision who to visit during the holidays, one family often feels betrayed. This is especially true if grandchildren are involved.

Everyone wants to belong no matter the price. Those who do not fall in line in the family are considered disloyal and treated as such by the larger family system. They are commonly referred to as a "Black Sheep." Those excluded for being disloyal or different in some way pay a heavy price for their longing and desire to do things differently.

Generation after generation in any family has a strong set of rules. These rules must be followed to keep everyone in order to keep the family stable as their position in society. Some of the rules are under the guise of traditions. If the family has any dark, dirty secrets anyone who speaks the truth is viewed as the enemy or betrayer.

Guilt and shame are powerful tools to manipulate and keep everyone quiet. Exclusion from your family can feel like death on an emotional level. This happens in the animal kingdom as well. It is instinctual to survive in all species. Staying together in a pack, school or family unit increases the rate of survival. It takes tremendous courage and strength to go against the grain and express yourself in a different way than the rest of your family.

Family loyalists may ostracize and reject anyone who does not remain loyal to the family. Inclusion feels good and exclusion does not. This happens in societies from primitive to modern since the dawn of time. Wars are fought over perceived differences in tribes, nations, religions and countries. The interaction in society and the world has a deep impact on family systems as well.

Loyalty holds power and conflict equally. The first inner conflict starts with mother and father and their respective family systems. If there is any tension between the mother and father, the child feels the energy even if it is in utero. If a pregnancy was not planned and the baby is unwanted, the undercurrent of feeling unwanted is passed to the child. It is a win/lose situation. It is a win because the child receives life but a loss because life is complicated and full of inner conflict. The child will have inner conflict about belonging its entire life just over conception.

The deepest truth is life was granted. Your connection to your family may be tenuous but this life is your experience. You may manifest what you want in this physical reality even if you were given an emotional gift basket of guilt, shame, betrayal, grief, and loss. It is up to your individuated spirit and courageousness to find your way out of the labyrinth of your family system. The most hard and fast rule is obey and you are in. Disobey and you are out. The ultimate choice is yours.

As you age it becomes an internal battle for personal integrity and autonomy over collective approval. You will always belong to your family system no matter whether you betray their values or not. Betrayal and loyalty are some of the most complex rules anyone in our species has to encounter. Your decisions can be viewed as positive or negative by others. Sometimes we have to suffer to belong. It is all part and parcel of what is expected.

The conundrum you face is being loyal to yourself and your personal truth or being loyal to others who will feel betrayed if your loyalty is based elsewhere. Are we willing to bear the price of being shunned for not being loyal to the group? Can you be strong in the face of it by being loyal to yourself even if it goes against the tide? You have the power of choice to keep your own integrity and autonomy intact.

Ask yourself these questions to open up your internal dialog:

- Who are you loyal to and why?

- Do you pay a price for loyalty?

- What is that price?

- Are you loyal to yourself?

- Do you pay a price for personal integrity?

- How do you handle the dynamics of loyalty and betrayal internally with your family, socially, in business or other personal relationships?

- How do you cope best?

- Are you happy being perceived as betraying anyone by putting yourself first?

- Do you have guilt for being who you are?

- How do you handle guilt or blame from others over your choices?

The interesting thing about loyalty and betrayal is how guilt and shame are used to keep you in line from a very young age. Organized religion has capitalized on this for centuries. They have the supreme guilt of God judging you if you do not follow their doctrine. Pray for forgiveness and absolution if you waiver from the rules of this dogma with guilt and shame.

Those who choose to disagree with any social system also have the power to alter or create an evolution of consciousness for the very species that represses them. Whether you consider Martin Luther King Jr.'s stance on civil rights and racial equality, Christopher Columbus' belief that the world was round, or Mahatma Gandhi's mission of peace, it is really the dynamics of the macrocosm of life on numerous levels. This is true in all families.

There are prices internally or externally for silence and for speaking up. It may be alive in the perpetrator who cannot live with him or herself over those they victimized and in the victims who are cowered into silence. The secrets will kill them too. Every person on this earth is affected by these invisible dynamics. We "betray" our parents by doing life differently, like our parents did to their parents and so on. However, it is part of a larger cycle that ties into our soul mission beyond the constraints of our family system.

28.

THE REAL PRICE
OF BELONGING
TO FAMILY SYSTEMS

Constellations reveal dynamics emerging in unique individual souls at the deepest of levels. You agreed to be incarnated into human form. This comes with a built-in family made up of many generations. Your family can give you the largest lessons, give you the biggest gifts and endow you with many challenges. You learn survival skills and are tested all throughout your life especially in your younger years.

The newer deeper dynamic is that we incarnate on our Spiritual mission but become supremely distracted by the family system. Belonging takes precedence over the reason. It is all part of our destiny and fate and sadly that is rarely honored by members of families. It is a grand cycle everyone partakes in and we learn and study during each incarnation.

29.

THE DYNAMICS
OF SELF BETRAYAL

You incarnated as an innocent, pure, new being for your latest lifetime of study and learning in the earth realm. When you were born, you had a mission for your life. However, you may have gotten distracted by the high jinks of your family system. To survive you may have overridden your soul's mission to belong. You may have lost who you were to win favor with mother, father, siblings or grandparents. The pressure to fit in can be enormous.

The world can corrupt you in addition to your family system. You are not privy to the deep undercurrent of give and take happening on the soul level. This is where self-betrayal is masked as love.

One of the biggest ironies of all is that most pregnancies are not planned. Most babies are a by product of orgasmic animal instinct that takes over with a careless desire to be sexual. More often than not, people are powerless in face of these impulses. These strong forces of life ensure the continuation of the species. They create both intentional and unintentional parents. It does not matter if there is an intention to marry or not. Their fate and destiny is sealed by the creation of new life which forms an eternal bond. The baby is the proof they will be tied together forever.

Once you are pregnant or get someone pregnant, the decision to have a child is made psychologically, mentally and emotionally. This is true even if you have a miscarriage or abortion. The bond may not come to fruition on the physical level but it is a significant part of your life eternally. The baby created in the union is an innocent coming to check out what is going on with life. The creative impulse expressed as humans is to seek new creation with curiosity and vigor. Lessons will be learned with each experience.

You were meant to be. After all, you are here and reading this book so it all worked out in your favor. Even if your parents did not want you, the conditions for you to be born were perfect and under a higher force larger than your parents. If you look at sexuality and life itself, you can see the forces that are bigger than you or your parents. You were incarnated for a reason. You are a child of the universe and placed in your family system at birth.

To be empowered by the fact that the Universe conspired to have you present and here for a specific reason, it is up to you what to do with this gift. You may believe it is a curse. There will be many other lifetimes to learn and get it right. Until that incarnation occurs, give up the struggle. It really takes too much life force. Sometimes the very thing you are struggling for makes you lose. You can believe you won, but you lost. You may "win the battle but lose the war," but at what cost?

If you continually "need" the negatives of the family history and feel victimized by life and your parents, it is time to move up and out of the past. If you feel trapped there is a way out. Constellations can give you an overview of your place in the family and the larger system. When you are in the right birth order including abortions and miscarriages, you can release a lot of negative energy that may have you feel trapped.

You always have the power and choice. Winning on a deeper level makes true victory all the sweeter.

30.

SELF-SABOTAGE 101

I've facilitated or witnessed many Constellations that exhibit a dance of polar opposites. Even after almost two decades of facilitation I'm always astounded at the deep, subtle dynamic contained within the self-sabotage paradigm. Whether we choose to view it as an internal or external, aggressor or victim dynamic is beside the point. It remains two polarized forces with different nuances of the same chain forged by fate. Fortunately, Constellation Healing Experiences afford us the opportunity to objectively see the dynamics at work internally and externally simultaneously.

Science is now discovering that PTSD and similarly complex dynamics are inherited epigenetically without directly having the traumatic experience. Our DNA carries the unprocessed dramas and traumas quite efficiently. It wasn't safe during the traumatic event to do so, which contributed to our psychological survival. Whatever isn't processed can be genetically passed on to the next generation to resolve. Through utilizing Healing Constellations one can speed up the process of centuries of unresolved issues in a mere hour. Considering the stage was set one or two centuries ago by ancestors we never met, but shared by epigenetic experiences in a place and time that ceases to exist in real time, but remains seemingly in suspended animation in "Eternal Time."

The emerging science of epigenetics applied to a Constellation Healing experience

Our present lives are greatly affected by the genetic heritage of the energetic field which surrounds our physical DNA. Current scientific studies are discovering that a vast amount of information is stored within, regarding the collective experiences of past generations, which influence us in the present.

Think of it as an energetic remembrance of the experiences, places and times they lived while casting a shadow onto the future – ours as well as theirs. After all, we are a summation of their DNA, and, as science has shown, we share it simultaneously with all members of our ancestry, both living and dead, regardless of time or space. In a Constellation Healing Experience we use the attributes of this timeless, quantum manifestation to our advantage.

During this amazing process, we have complete access to the hidden realms of our ancestral past. This allows us to share the experience and work with those collective dynamics contained within the life force of each individual in our family system's lineage. In doing so, we find tremendous healing as well as inner and outer peace. It also gives us profound insight, a renewed strength and determination to embrace our life, our shared past, with acceptance and clarity. By realizing that we are supported by our entire family lineage, we are able to face our future in a more positive and connected way. Truly, we are standing on the shoulders of giants. Omniscience is ours for the taking, as we are the ones they've been waiting for. We are their dreams coming true.

How parents can use Constellation Healing

For a parent, a Constellation Experience has amazing value in revealing and healing any problem that your child may be experiencing. Simply put, any issue that your child may be having in life may not even be his or hers to carry. When a parent attends a Constellation workshop, an adult surrogate is used to represent the child (or issue), and the epigenetic field shows us what is really affecting him or her at the deepest level. Generally, hidden dynamics are revealed which are at the root of the problem or issue. For example given the multigenerational nature of family patterns, such issues may have been passed down from their grandparents' generation. As the energetic truth of the real issue reveals itself, even those who are not physically present also benefit from the healing process. When the energy is released, a larger family field of awareness is affected, healing all family members (present and past) at the deepest and most profound levels. This work essentially dispels the unfinished business of the past, resulting in a clearer future for all concerned.

After experiencing a Constellation workshop, you may have a renewed sense of compassion for yourself, your parents and the innocence of your child, who will then be less impacted by the family's "negative" dynamics. Helping to lift those energetic pressures is one of the best things a parent can do to insure his or her child's success in life. By neutralizing the traumas of those who came before, those traumas will not need to be repeated by future generations, and we are able to transform and enhance the possibilities for what is yet to come. What better place can there be for anyone to start in life then with a clean slate and open eyes.

We are the "dreams come true" of our ancestral past. We are living the dream of a better day and a hopeful future that they wished for and longed to see. If they did not get that opportunity, we have another chance to do so in their memory — which is the greatest honor we can give them. Living in a place of presence, joy, happiness, and success is the highest achievement we can attain in our short time here on earth. We owe it to the next generation. Let's help them become the healthy, well-functioning adults they are meant to be.

We are all participants in the Wheel of Life, each with their own role to learn and grow. If you go to a supermarket and buy meat or any other animal product, behind the scenes that beef or animal product purchased faced a brutal murder at the slaughter house. What we ingest in civilized society removes us from the perpetrator energy used to slaughter our food. Although animals in the wild live each moment of "kill or be killed," we have the convenience of others doing the dirty work for us. The violence is behind the scenes and we see a bright red muscle behind the cellophane on our grocer's shelf. If there is ever a shortage of food or water from any supply chain breakdown you'll see how fast our survival instincts become roused. The fight for food will start after the looting ends. The motivation to kill or steal to eat will come to the forefront of our consciousness. As human animals we'll kill to eat, kill to live, and kill to reproduce. Of course it's all masked by civilization. The laws of the jungle do not stop once awakened. Notice how angry you become in any grocery store if someone bumps into your shopping cart? Our instinct or fight or flight is lurking right there. Finding a parking space close to the store? There it is again…Waiting in a long line for a cashier to pay… it's there too. Now you see how thin the veneer of civilization really is. So what do these simple examples show us?

- That we are hard wired for aggression, violence or perpetrator energy at a moment's notice.

- It comes out in any situation where a threat is perceived.

- We do not judge it as good or bad unless someone else is violent or a victim.

All living things will fight to the death to live or play dead to survive

We may seem separate from animals but at the deepest of levels we're not. Society and civilization insulates us nicely into an unconscious slumber. We are so easy to control.

The true opiate of the masses; easy food supply, television, and fearful news. If you look at war on earth you'll see fear for eons. Most wars are fought over beliefs and the idea that God is on our side making a righteous perpetration against the lesser of an opposing state or nation.

Interestingly, in Constellations, Aggressor/Perpetrator energy has subtly different invisible dynamics. Very often we find the perpetrators as weak and the victims strong. In other cases the aggressor/perpetrator is tied and manipulated to kill through a false ideology therefore they are the victims of false beliefs of unstable leaders. However, it makes their actions no less evil. We can separate the dynamics in intimate details as well as the victim side. Aggressors and perpetrators tend to feel something is missing within and they think they can get it by overpowering their targeted victim group. Feeling empty and soulless, they mindlessly react, making the whole ordeal futile. Sure they sometimes get honors but then they live with the guilt of their atrocities. Their children very often represent the victims so there is no escape for all concerned. Both the victims and their killers suffer greatly. The illusion of external safety is a just that, an illusion.

In the animal world the strongest killers eat and reproduce better offspring, becoming the bloodthirsty king or queen of the hill. The gene pool survives as the weak are literally eaten. Sometime it's just for water or food and nothing else. The environment has a lot to do with these dynamics of survival and blood thirst. More food and water = less violence. All creatures inherently want to be fat and happy. They ruthlessly kill to achieve it. It's the Law of the Jungle at play within all species. We as humans are cooperative like insect colonies, each having their job to serve the whole. Life has millions of dynamics interacting all at once seemingly with reckless abandon. It is how we deal with the fallout that matters. And please understand, I am not endorsing violence or destruction in any way. My goal is to expand your view, and see how the machinations affect you, your family, and ancestors. The more we understand, the more we can have compassion and equanimity.

Each of us is involved in this dance, at various times on either side of the spectrum. As Gandhi stated so clearly, "An eye for and eye, makes everyone blind!" I want you to comprehend the greater and subtler forces at play; an unconsciously righteous aggressor or victim creates repetition of the cycle. Righteousness is a key sign of a hidden perpetrator dynamic starting to emerge. On either side it is dark energy. Being right, or thinking you are aligned with your perceived God or Savior doesn't make it okay. It's a psychological defense to clear the guilty conscience of any wrongdoing. Both victims and perpetrators must be seen and honored for the cycle end.

Constellations afford us the luxury of transforming the invisible forces that we are at the mercy of but didn't create. The process allows us to see many dynamics in a new way with objectivity.

Life is a bloodthirsty amoral force, it doesn't care about anything other than to survive at all cost and move forward.

Try to see life as a kelly green snake quietly slithering unpredictably in bright green grass. It never stops to look behind, just moves forward to its unknown destination blending in, just like us. Humans, being conscious, have memory to reflect and reminisce. We are cognizant of time and space in a way that other beings are not. It's simultaneously a blessing and a curse.

There is trauma on either side of the Karmic Coin. Memories haunt us. It is as if the original events never die but are stored for safekeeping until danger has passed and it's all sorted out. In a lot of cases, trauma repeats intragenerational in order to honor the suffering of those that came before. It seems there's a "soul camaraderie" for interpreting life in the same way as our ancestors. It's a way to belong by having a shared experience.

It's very important to try to stay neutral and let the Karmic Coin roll and travel its own way.

I believe the Yin & Yang Symbol (a black teardrop with a small white circle in its center or white teardrop with a small black circle in its center) is a great metaphor. To translate the symbolic meaning; in the light there is a small element of dark that will grow into the white teardrop transforming it into the black one. The black one will reverse in the same way, its light will grow internally transforming it into a white teardrop, with a small dark circle at its center. You can see both light and dark components of duality are really one and the same. There's a small amount of aggressor/perpetrator energy in the light which will transform one day and vice versa. They are intertwined like twins in a womb. They grow and change to learn what the opposite is, thereby learning everything. This is how the Wheel of Life works and moves forward in time. Darkness creates light and light creates darkness as, Yin to Yang and Yang to Yin. Duality powers it all equally so it can move forward into the future. There is no reverse.

If we can take a minute to stop and witness these bigger forces of life, then we can see how we are at the effect of them. We can see how we too embody aggressor/perpetrator or victim forces in our own lives. It doesn't have to be anything as explosive as murder. It can be quite small and subtle. Take for example smoking. Most people know it isn't good for their health, They are called "coffin nails" for good reason. Ask any smoker why they do not stop, "one day I will... after this last cigarette." Procrastination is one way we victimize ourselves.

We do it. We know it's bad. We do it anyway. We knowingly risk the consequences. For example:

- A diabetic who eats sugar

- An obese person who overeats

- A drug addict who keeps using

- A shopaholic who keeps shopping

There's a hidden, self-destructive impulse in each of these common behaviors. Those who perpetrate against themselves become victims of their own behavior. This explains why people often say "you're your own worst enemy."

We each embody these dynamics in the minute ways yet we blame the tobacco companies, our parents, our spouse, and anything outside of ourselves so as not to assume personal responsibility for our self-destructive actions, ensuring that we remain a self-righteous victim. This self-sabotage we deal with on a daily basis prevents us from moving forward. We can conveniently blame external forces up until our deathbed. But blaming outside forces really doesn't empower us to be the successful, happy adults we were meant to be.

Four questions to ask yourself:

1. How do you self-sabatoge in your life?

2. Do you know why can't you stop doing it?

3. Who do you blame?

4. If there were no external force to blame what inner changes would you make?

Being empowered doesn't mean you have to become an aggressive perpetrator. With presence you can choose to be fully conscious of a neutral yet assertive, middle state. You can make choices from a middle place rather than the extreme place.

Here's the victim/perpetrator dynamic in a nutshell. Any victim who feels superior to their perpetrator has the element of perpetrator energy in their self-righteousness. Most perpetrators already feel they're better and that the victims deserve to be victims.

When we can embrace the duality of light and dark, then we'll have a chance to be empowered and transform both our ancestral and current family system. With presence, we can become internally aware of these dynamics, allowing us to make better choices.

Most people who feel victimized by an external aggressor or overpowered by perpetrator energy have one thing in common, they lose their choice and power. If you boil trauma down to its lowest common denominator, it really is about loss of personal power and autonomy. Being overpowered and having your choices manipulated or eliminated is a core issue for many people throughout their lives.

Does life create this on a very deep level to test our resolve? Is life's singular goal to build strength and resilience? Does life do this to make us strong to survive the onslaught outside of our family system when we leave home? Does life force us to be tenacious as we strive to survive?

Every Perpetrator or Aggressor was a Victim First

We have the strength, even as a child, to survive even horrific traumas. Thus, we have the strength to heal it, let it go, and leave it in the past.

In Constellations there is often a wall of resistance that has to be broken through. Luckily attendees volunteer in the role of representatives portraying the client. So the working client is able to be objective about their subjectivity in their role. Constellations create a living multidimensional laboratory of sorts — to try on behaviors or see beliefs in a new way. Enabling these new insights and thought forms to come through makes room for tenderness. Deep painful wounds can be healed within our souls once and for all.

One of three biggest stumbling blocks is that victimized clients were forced to say "yes" to traumatizing events, thereby having their "no" taken away. It could be construed that any and all victims on many levels lose their personal autonomy along with the ability to say yes or no.

The mind set that results from trauma creates a situation where free will and choice seem to be absent in many areas of life. School, work, friendships, romantic relationships, as well as relationships with siblings and parents. The aggressor/perpetrator invades the victim's space and life against their will. Help is often sorely needed to get their ability to make choices in an empowering way (especially women). Reacquainting them with yes and no is a good place to start. This provides strength, empowerment, and autonomy simultaneously.

Questions to help you think, grow, and learn:

1. Who victimized you and how were you victimized?

2. When did this happen?

3. How did you cope?

4. Were you forced to say "yes" or be silent?

6. Can you now say "no" to the perpetrator?

7. Can you stand in your power knowing that this was your fate and destiny with this person?

8. Do you carry them in your pain as well?

If you feel that there is more to process, a Constellation to target that specific aspect of the issue can help bring it to resolution and release. The deepest helping occurs when we can fully let it go and let it be in our past. Doing so also gives us a new-found strength to move forward.

The "all-knowing field" teaches us that the victim, even a small child, actually has more strength that any aggressor or perpetrator they encounter. Most perpetrators are damaged and emotionally weak, and their illusion of strength comes from trying to over-power their own unresolved feelings of victimization. They too carry the pain of what was done to them. They react from an almost trance-like state, unconsciously condemned to repeat victimizing others in order to feel powerful. Ironically, most perpetrators say they couldn't control their actions because a force overtook them to which they felt helpless. This is why it is so important to be cognizant of how past events affect us in the present. When we allow our past to continue to make us feel victimized, we run the risk of trying to balance those feelings by manifesting perpetrator energy ourselves.

And again, we don't just react by perpetrating against others. Sometimes the most subtle victimization we do to ourselves. We sabotage our own progress because we don't feel worthy of moving forward unencumbered. We wonder who we'd be if we didn't have the burdens that slow or stop us.

But I can tell you this: it's worth finding out.

Saboteur isn't just a less-than-satisifying Hitchcock film; it's a less-than-satisfying way to live.

31.

GROWING BEYOND BETRAYAL

"Every generation pays for its survival with self-betrayal."

What was your original mission? What did you come here to learn? What fate and destiny did you agree to? Was being part of your family system your only goal this incarnation? Is your family a great distraction or test to keep your soul mission alive? Do others cause interference, pushing you off that path?

The mission is to keep your path intact. You have the power to win when you walk away with love. It is empowering as an adult to leave on your own terms. At the very least, your integrity will be intact. As an adult you have survived your childhood. You need to set healthy boundaries. Fate and destiny still rule the day evident in the chaos all around you.

You always have room to make a new choice whether to be empowered or a victim to your life. That is a choice you can make day by day and moment by moment. The Universe supports you either way without judgment. Your ego wracks you enough between the battle of mind and soul. Just as you did at your conception use this truth and power of the present moment to guide you to choose to life, and live the life you were meant to.

Family systems have deep tentacles with tools of betrayal, guilt, shame, sadness, and anger at their disposal to push the buttons needed for you to conform and belong. When you do take a stand, you will start to see the hooks come out and try to reel you into the role they believe is right for you. If you can observe this happening as if there's glass on a wall in front of you to deflect their hooks into your gut, heart or mind, you will be better for it. This personal boundary of power has been there since day one.

As a child you may have betrayed who you are to survive. You did it with a mixture of love and regret. Now it is time to take your life back. Who are you without your family? Define yourself in a new way; do not reject the past and those who came before but include them on your own terms. This is true empowerment. It is a rite of passage and those rights have freedoms evolving with you moment by moment. You can move past your childhood because it will always be with you. Step into your own individuated power now. Find the meaning of your life and what you desire to experience. Your life and future depends on it.

Acceptance: This means seeing whatever truth is shown. You may just accept the fate or destiny of the group or individual without regret. By letting go of past events that can never be changed, you can change the future.

Forgiveness: Unlike most spiritual practices, this work does not encourage you to forgive others. Instead this act of "bigness" forces you to carry weight that is not yours, further perpetuating disorder. Your parents are adults who have the strength to carry the responsibility of their own actions. You do not have to take on what is not yours to carry. You are an adult letting your parent be adults responsible for their own fate. This way you are not a victim either.

Victim/Perpetrator: It is important to discover who the real victim was as well as the perpetrator. Things are not always what they seem. The official story may cover up the "energetic" reality of the situation, especially with regard to cases of exclusion. There are also instances of violence where the roles shift as instantaneously as the shot of a gun. It can make the victim the real perpetrator and the perpetrator the victim. Again, they are the two edges of the same systemic sword. Be aware and be sensitive.

32.
THE BAGGAGE
OF GUILT

Guilt and shame are very powerful tools used to keep us in line. They are used by families, society, cultures, and religions. It works well and has made commercialized, organized religion very wealthy. The mere fact that natural sexual impulses are labeled a "sin" says it all. Even the books of the Bible which originally emphasized our relationship to the Holy Spirit were edited to be more about adherence to the doctrines of the church. And some, such as the Gospel of Mary Magdalene, were excised completely. It may have been *The Greatest Story Ever Told*, but it wasn't the whole story.

For centuries, most of our societal and cultural beliefs around morality have been reinforced, consciously and subconsciously, in just this manner. These manufactured thought forms have affected all levels of society, not to mention all forms of politics. "My God is better than your God" is the implication. All of these beliefs are intentionally engineered and designed with moral structures to keep us in our place. After all, who are we to decide what's right and wrong?

This manufactured structure fuels each family system to keep in lockstep with these contrivances of manipulation.

Imbedded in the cultural underpinnings of society, sex in all forms is considered a sin. Our biological impulses are deemed "wrong." The fact that people internalize guilt and shame for doing what is natural is the real sin. We are not allowed to trust our unique flow and impulses if they are not condoned by the church, society or our family's moral code of behavior.

In a family system it gets much more complex. Innocence, guilt, betrayal, anger, and sadness all go hand in hand. Every person is born innocent. Everyone is taught to betray themselves to show love symbolically. This might show itself by someone saying "If you love me, you will..." This is a threat because if their conditions are not met, it proves love does not exist.

Guilt follows betrayal as yet another tool for control for the battle for your soul. Shame follows close behind. These efforts, no matter how misguided, are the last ditch efforts to wield power by a manipulator. The manipulator does not have any concern on how those threats affect you. This is true of mothers, fathers, grandparents, school teachers, classmates, spouses, romantic partners, and friends. It works on all levels of society and all cultures.

The machine has been very well oiled for centuries with a hidden goal of keeping people down at all cost or at least controlled into submission.

What happened to unconditional love, nurturing, approval, self-esteem, and all the positive emotions? Usually you receive tidbits of positive but giant servings of the negative. It is no wonder why there is so much "Dis-Ease" and violence in the world on a daily basis. You may not be able to reconcile your real impulses from the morally ordered ones. Hence it is an internal conflict projected externally.

You started off as joyful and innocent until people in your life used guilt and shame to control you. All of this happened in your formative years. Many wonder why their lives are so difficult. Is your life difficult? You cannot change others but you can take a stand for yourself through honesty, love, presence, and compassion for those tangled in the web of deceit. Wish them well, disengage, and turn away towards freedom.

They may think guilt and shame are the only way they can connect. This, of course, is a delusion. You have the power to leave the guilt and shame with those who imposed it on you. Extricating yourself from it is no small task, but is the best thing to do. Freedom is on the other side.

It is a great lesson to learn about the delicate, intimate systemic dynamics of guilt; what we carry, and its personal cost. In truth you suffer for others out of love. Systemically guilt takes the place of a healthy loving bond.

This guilt is subtle and invasive. How dare someone "do life" in a different way; dare to make themselves happy, not care how others will suffer if they do not pay the price of conformity. These insidious dynamics play out in every family system. It is an ancient dysfunctional habit that few have the courage to challenge lest they be rejected or excluded for upending the status quo.

All of the players in your ancestral chain agreed to the rules of this game called life. It seems guilt equals power and many use it to prove that they are loved. Fear and guilt lead to shame. These tools are very powerful ways to change someone's behavior through manipulation. As a child you may have been victim of these powerful yet negative tools to teach you about life and your place in your family system. Do not forget there are rules of belonging that are deep and unspoken.

"Everyone must suffer in a certain way because this is the way it is and has always been." However, as an adult you have a choice. You can take a stand for yourself. You can keep your personal integrity, as uncomfortable as it may be, intact. Be present and do not take the bait of manipulative guilt or shame. Do not let others force you to be helpless. Be the empowered person you were meant to be.

Constellations offer you a way out. It is an objective way to see the slithering secret dynamics at work that keep you entangled and unhappy just like all your family members before.

You can still belong but it can be on your own terms. Airing out those hidden secrets bring a much-needed breath of fresh air to most families. Let those who manipulate take responsibility of their actions. You may to take a risk to be rejected if you are to own your power. But if you don't, you are a slave to the negative, projected emotions of others. Once guilt is felt and processed for what it is, you can be free of it and move forward in your future. Can you let others be trapped in a web of their own design and just love them in spite of their entrapment?

Will you be courageous enough to stand free and set an example for your family and community, if not the world? Leave it behind with those who own it and use it. Move forward with ease as it was never yours to carry. Regain your innocence and freedom by honoring and loving those entangled behind you.

After all is said and done, guilt is a band-aid for someone else's pain. Ironically they are probably not even alive anymore, yet their reactions live on. Everyone is strong enough to handle the truth. When under duress try and remember, guilt enslaves you but the truth sets you free.

33.

INNOCENCE, FREEDOM, AND PERSONAL POWER ARE YOUR BIRTHRIGHT

Can you handle the weight and responsibility? Yes you can! The same energy it took to be enslaved is the same energy that sets you free. Your existence is most likely a result of the sexual pleasure of your parents. You have a body, therefore you belong. This is your birthright. Anything other than that is for your elders to carry.

When you are not true to yourself, you can become resentful and angry with your situation or towards people in your family. Your anger can also fester and be intensified with guilt for feeling the way you do. You could say you are fostering neurotic codependency and not real love. Real love is honest and pure truth in the present moment. Symbolic love is based on pleasing others. The latter will force you to communicate in the most dysfunctional way which perpetuates the problem.

Constellations seek the real truth by "opening the curtain," to reveal what remained unspoken. You are so much stronger than you think. You are capable of hearing the truth. Lies and deceit are the deadly faces that feed on guilt and shame disguised as love.

One of the biggest uses for guilt is power to control

others. The person who wields the power expects loyalty. The desire to belong may override the price you need to pay. You may lie to yourself and stay in the situation and stay in dysfunctional family dynamics. These are the dynamics that are passed from generation to generation and frequently taught as an expert survival skill set.

This can become a tragedy of generational proportions. The good news is you have survived and can move forward in spite of it.

We see how often guilt is driven underground and looks like loyalty to the family system. Loyalty becomes a substitute for love. It's time for "do as I say, not do as I do. If you love me you will..."

Family guilt also becomes political as well, used to win favor and play people against each other. It is an overt or covert way to make someone feel loved or prove they are loved. More often than not it is a false assumption that leads to continual lies and deceit. Everyone pretends to care about someone else's feelings more than their own. One person may win but everyone loses in the long run from the unreal connections and the lack of authentic permission to exist and belong as they authentically are.

Think of the freedom of expression in children. They will say exactly what is going on in their mind. You might hear a young kid say "I don't like you!" The adults go into a panic that the truth is out. They try to stifle it so no one's feelings will be hurt. Parents may even shame the child for his or her spontaneous honesty. The child learns to be quiet and suppress the truth. In most cultures and in previous eras, speaking freely was not considered acceptable behavior.

In Constellations the truth often comes out in its most raw, honest form. Those who suffered from not being seen are revealed. Their truth is voiced through the representative who is put into that role. The representative may feel a shift in energy like relief for finally putting a voice to the pain. The

Constellation allows the suffering to remain with that person. It is your ancestor's "choice," manifested in the representative, whether to hold on to it or release it. Either way the energy is not rolling forward through the generations toward you.

This is the best way to disentangle yourself from the unhealthy lineage. Constellations are a way to stand in truth and see and accept things as they really are or as the really were. It is a clear and clean way to be free of negative entanglements and yet maintain deep connection without neurotic, codependent trappings. The cruel irony is that we were forced into loyalty for all the wrong reasons.

The irony is that you never had to pay a price to belong. Your birth into the system affords you the connection to your family. You paid a price to keep others happy, at deep personal cost, yet you did not have to.

If you boil guilt down to its lowest common denominator or essence, it is merely the resistance you have to say "No." If you are not saying "No" to avoid hurting someone's feelings, you are denying your true authentic self. You then feel guilty for not being honest. This reflects how you are personally and systemically entangled. Dishonesty at its core is pretending to be love.

34.

A SHORT ESSAY TO ENCOURAGE YOU TO LIVE YOUR LIFE

This essay is written to encourage you to live a guilt free life. You will have a new boundary which includes that saying "No" is OK. It is designed to give you courage.

Be loyal to yourself now. Others will follow. Be honest. Create trust and respect. We are born with the inherent ability to be honest. We become corrupted when we mask our honest so that we can feel like we belong in our families.

All family system members were once young, new, fresh, and innocent. When the affect of hiding the truth is shown to them, many people can recognize what was once lost and replaced by guilt and shame. If you can do this, you will get back to your innocence. Allow those who manipulate by theatrical meltdowns to do so while you remain protected by remaining in Presence. Witness and love them unconditionally. Model your caring for them by being honest.

Love does not mean appeasing.

Love is not coercion.

True love is not manipulation.

Love is not guilt and guilt is not love.

Love is accepting all traits as they are. It is all part of life.

Stand strong and tall knowing you got it. Then wait and watch for the reactions. Resist the temptation to weaken yourself to make others appear strong.

35.

TRUTH OR CONSEQUENCES

Your Soul, though strong, is as delicate as a blooming flower. And like a flower, it can collapse and dry up waiting to be watered and nurtured. But even if it seems to have stopped blooming, you can bring it back to life with the right nutrients of trust, unconditional love, and truth. It can find and regain its vitality and strength to reopen to its beautiful grandeur. There is often an amazing amount of vitality contained within the Soul's life force even when it seems stifled by problems or riddled with conflict. The energy trapped within the hidden dysfunction, when released, is the same energy that can be used to heal and resolve that dysfunction.

The key lies in being present and tuning in to the deeper conflicts. When we tap into the field of consciousness, we are able to determine what needs to be released. And though the majority of the work takes place in the energetic realm, the results have a profound effect on the physical plane.

Often, we find that certain family members are trying protect others in the family from the deepest pains and alleged wrongdoings of their ancestors. Unfortunately, by trying to distract from a painful truth, they are also distracting from a possible resolution. Grief, guilt, and shame can remain in a family for generations, causing greater pain than the truth that's being hidden. Once a secret is out in the open, it no longer has the power to affect us subconsciously. Getting the chance to say what was never able to be said has tremendous freeing power. "My grandfather was a murderer." "My grandmother had a miscarriage." These are all statements that can bring clarity and closure. Denial has unintended consequences. Acceptance, without judgement, can be that missing piece that can disentangle us. And sometimes a "Good-bye" or "I love you" is all that is needed.

There is no right or wrong — only truth.

To reiterate: The energy contained in any dysfunctional or knee-jerk response is the same energy that propels healing through awareness. Consciousness knows no limits or boundaries. It will go to the deepest depths or highest highs. On a soul level, we all crave light, truth, and resolution. What is astounding is that we will wait for years in a state of suspended animation for the right conditions to arise. And the longer we wait, the more stuck we become. It is possible, however, for us to "jump start" those conditions right now by addressing what is blocking us in an honest and direct way.

I have long contended that there is a correlation between what we carry emotionally and what we carry physically. Could "dis-ease" be a physical expression of unresolved or unexpressed emotions? Could this body that we incarnated into be carrying any of the guilt, pain, shame, or grief of those who came before? We share their DNA. Perhaps that's not all. Might we also be carrying the scars of their unresolved wounds into our future?

Not only is it possible, it's very likely. I see many cases where the unfinished issues in the family system take their toll on the following generation. The study of epigenetics is helping to provide further evidence of how emotional components of the past can trigger physical responses in our bodies today.

People are very sensitive, emotional, psycho-spiritual beings. What if disease is how we carry unspoken truths? What if by facing them we could change the course of any negative somatic influence? In other words, when we can accept the truth of what was, dark ancestral secrets and all, we free ourselves from having to carry anything emotionally or physically that isn't ours to carry. When we stand in truth, we send out an intention of health. And when we're emotionally healthy, hopefully the physical will follow.

36.
VIEWING YOUR SILENT MOVIE

We all come from a long line of ancestors. Each generation reacts to the movie that life manifests during their life time. Some of us endured the tragedy of war, starvation or famine. Others enjoyed wealth, success, and good fortune.

In acting, when actors experience the internal aspect of a role or character, they call it accessing "Sense Memory." Our ancestral lineage has this very same memory encoded epigenetically in our bodies. It can seem like an ever repeating movie playing over and over generation after generation. You may see these parallels in your own ancestral lineage. Ask yourself:

- What sequel are you being asked to star in?

- Will you play the same role as your ancestor?

- Will your sequel also be a tragedy or can you rewrite the script to have a positive ending?

- Do you have a choice what kind of movie you want to experience?

- Is there a way to see what invisible role you are playing?

The movie of your past is a silent movie. Today you live in a 3D Technicolor world with surround sound. However, both your movies are running simultaneously within you; one in the background, the other in the foreground. One affects the other. Constellations enable us to gain access to this silent background movie. We gain access to the incomplete dramas by viewing them from the audience as an external experience. Other people are used as representative or surrogates of our family members. This exposes issues that may be affecting our life.

In a Constellation, the scene initially unfolds as a mystery. No one in the room knows what it is about, what the plot is, or what will be revealed just like in a play or a movie. The representatives express both physical and emotional feelings they are able to access once they are on the "stage" or in the Field of Consciousness. Incomplete scenes are completed. Long forgotten incidents, frozen in time, are revealed.

A seasoned facilitator guides the session. The client and facilitator know what may potentially show up. They intuitively add representatives to play the historic parts as the story unfolds. The Field of Consciousness will also activate and indicate the direction of the scene that wants to be revealed.

All participants need to be very flexible. The most sacred, delicate scene that is revealed to the client can become a profoundly healing experience. The silent film comes to life as a 3D "Talkie." The ancestors may open up about their pain through the representatives and voice that which was previously silent.

The facilitator's job is to observe and guide the story, helping it evolve to whatever completion feels right. The silent movie is allowed to be front and center instead of hiding in the background. The movements, words, emotions, and pain are supported and nurtured to transform and thus be accepted. This frees the client from the unfinished silent movie to create a new one during his or her lifetime while honoring those who came before. This allows the client's ancestors to know their suffering was not in vain. Life moved on. Their heritage moves forward in their posterity because of their ability to participate by proxy in the Constellation.

The goal of the facilitator is to bring the truth to light while helping bring resolution and completion to the silent movie as it is projected. After watching the movie, the person having the Constellation has seen the "director's cut" and can view it in a different way. Everyone in the room, including the ancestors being represented, is transformed. The energy being passed forward to the next generations shifts for the better.

When we have the courage to view the unseen footage we can change any *Nightmare on Elm Street* to an *It's A Wonderful Life*.

PART FIVE

SHOW TIME!

37.

CONSTELLATION LIFE STORIES: THREE CLIENTS

Consciousness knows no boundaries or limitations. It transcends time and space, just as an idea can be everywhere at once. This applies to the subconscious mind as well. Just as light is a physical property, it also contains a large spectrum of energy mostly unseen in its white hue. We may not always be aware of the impact our ancestors have upon our current lives, but their influence can be felt all the same.

Having facilitated thousands of constellation workshops over the years, I've encountered some intriguing and, frankly, horrific stories that seem pulled directly from the horror film headlines. And such traumas and dramas seem to have an unquestionably cinematic slant. My purpose in sharing some of these stories is to help you more fully understand the nature of the dysfunction at play in many family systems, often "hidden in plain sight." And yes, the names have been changed to protect the innocent.

Client Story #1: *Silence of the Lambs* **Live**

A wonderful new client came my way, and I immediately saw the light in her eyes. Yet as I read her family history, I discovered there had been imprisonment, sexual torture, and perverse abuse that would make Hannibal Lecter blush. (Clarice would have thrown up all over her cheap shoes just hearing about it.)

As her family constellation progressed, her family system appeared as silent, living corpses pretending to be alive. The grief and stagnancy was astounding. The representatives looked like zombies trapped in an infected Hell of their own making, tears streaming down their tormented faces. It was *Dawn of the Dead* meets Michael Jackson's *Thriller*. It appeared as if the entire ugly scenario had come back to victimize the poor girl all over again.

Yet, that was not her reaction. Low and behold, we could see that the only one who was not dead in this whole sordid group of zombies was the client herself, I'll call her Angel. And here she was, some thirty years later, sitting with me and watching in amazement as a group of total strangers embodied her family system with pinpoint accuracy. Terrifying as it was to watch (much less to have lived through), she had not become one of them. Despite horrific sexual abuse and imprisonment for most of her childhood, they had not poisoned her to the beauty and promise of life.

That truth had to be voiced, and it cut through the tension in the room like Norman Bates' knife. Angel had lived with a group of vampires who had fed on her for years, yet they had not sucked one drop of precious life out of her. She was as alive as you could get, and she was able to see that she was. Despite the sexual, emotional, and physical scars, she had survived. She may have known her story, but what had been unknown, even to her, was her strength.

Discovering this not only liberated her, it helped her to see, for the first time, that she was, and is, the strongest person in her entire family system. More importantly, it allowed her to let go of the past and leave her negative experiences to fate and destiny, freeing her from any subconscious desire to further serve the perpetrators in her family system.

The butterfly was able to soar from its cocoon, leaving her tortured past behind her. Angel was free at last.

(Incidentally, eight other participants in the constellation workshop that night had a history of sexual abuse in their own lives, and were finally able disentangle themselves from the fate of their own perpetrators, leaving the guilt and shame with them. A win for all.)

Angel is still doing great in her life and soaring to new heights knowing she was the strong one all along. The lambs may be silent, but the *Butterflies Are Free*!

Clarice Starling would be proud.

Client Story #2: *Rosemary's Baby* meets *Nightmare on Elm Street*

It was a heavy, dark case of multigenerational satanic worship and human sacrifice. It was a real life case that made *Eyes Wide Shut* look like a parlor game. I'll call the client Greta.

It's rare that I work with such dark cases, yet it is a challenge is to find the light that's hidden within the darkness. There is always a beacon hiding somewhere beneath the rubble. This tough case was not for the faint of heart, to say the least. However Greta wanted a better life and I'm glad I was available to help her. Her main goal was release from the daily obsessive blackness that emotionally consumed her life.

Much like Garbo, Greta now just "vanted" to be alone. Her privacy was her utmost concern. She wanted to feel safe. She wanted protection from her satanic perpetrator parents and grandparents who sought power and status through the darkest means imaginable. Tragically, they not only offered their first born for sacrifice but executed the first born in two consecutive generations. The grandmother did this for her first daughter and the surviving daughter did this as a mother to her first born, leaving the second born of each generation to cope with the horrific trauma and guilt. Death would have been easier than to survive such a *Nightmare on Elm Street* existence. Understandably, Greta wanted to work by means of a "distance constellation." She was still too terrified to attend a workshop in person. Nevertheless, with each constellation we did for her (and there were several) her fears were more and more eased, and her life kept improving considerably.

Remember, these are huge dynamics to carry, along with a heavy multi generational fate of the darkest order. No, I'm not like *The Devil's Advocate* where Al Pacino bargains with people's souls like a lawyer from *Hell on Earth*. (But enough about New York.) The good news is that Greta survived, and that the airing of the dynamics led to an emotional healing from a horrific real-life double feature worse than *The Exorcist* and *Rosemary's Baby* combined.

She was finally able to leave the guilt and shame with those to whom it belonged, thereby disentangling herself from their fates, their destinies, and their karmic lessons to learn. It was neither our purpose nor place to play *Exorcist* and try to cast out the seemingly inexplicable draw to satanism found within her family system. Still, the insights gained through her ancestral conscious field were remarkable. We learned as a group that they sought the light through darkness, much like trying to use coal as a prism to magnify what's hidden inside. (Just imagine Greta Garbo starring in *Coal Miner's Daughter*. In other words, what's wrong with this picture?)

Seriously though, like any family system, it turned out to be about multi generational grief and loss. The women were bearing the grief, guilt, and shame for the men who sought status and power in their Church of Satan. But as Jesus himself would say, "Forgive them, Father, for they know not what they do." Our goal was to free the client from suffering well into her late fifties from childhood traumas that would make Linda Blair's head spin. The "holy water" we use in any Constellation Healing Experience is unconditional love. Even for the darkest family systems, we honor and respect their fate (thereby leaving it with them) even if their actions seem crazy and murderous to us. Hate only begets more hate, and, having never been on the receiving end of unconditional love, it's the last thing they would expect.

Greta's healing continues to progress, and the challenge for her is not to see herself as the survivor of her past, but rather, to truly let it be in the past. Otherwise, it becomes *Groundhog Day*, reliving it over and over again. This is the tricky thing about trauma. It invites us to define ourselves as victims and we become *Frozen*, recreating our victimization over and over again, rather than stepping away and allowing ourselves to let it go.

But this is precisely what we need to do. Then we can move forward, back in touch with the inherent strength we received along with our creation, our hearts still intact, and willing to help manifest a better and happier future for ourselves. Hey, *It's a Wonderful Life* after all.

Client Story #3: *The Rise and Fall of the Third Reich* by way of *Schindler's List*

We'll call him Bob. His Constellation goal was simple. He wanted to sleep and hadn't been able to for his entire life.

During the work it was revealed that, even though he had never been in Auschwitz, his mother had been a prisoner there, and he was carrying her constant fear of impending doom at the hands of the Nazi guards. This had been a daily trauma for her, and what she had been unable to resolve in her own life was epigenetically (energetically) being carried on through him. Even though he hadn't suffered the direct traumatic experience himself, he was now wrestling with an "inherited" form of PTSD. Her DNA was in his DNA, and sharing the burden of her trauma, albeit subconsciously, was shown to be an important connection for him.

Each generation gets a new chance at life, but if you really stop and look at it, it is only ours because someone has shared it with us. Each snippet of our genome, after all, came from someone else. It is "borrowed," if you will, by each generation from the previous. Whether intended or not, each child receives the gift of life from his or her creators, along with a bit of "systemic baggage." But it's not the whole truth merely to say that it's passed on to the next generation. It also gets taken on by them, and it's done so out of love.

In Bob's case, his mother had survived a terrible fates, that of being imprisoned in a Nazi concentration camp. All the same, life was still able to pass through her thanks to the unstoppable power of sexuality and the desire to pass on the wonderful gift of life.

But it doesn't always start with a perfectly clean slate. There is often an echo of history in our DNA concerning what our ancestors experienced when that same DNA was part of them. Bob's lifelong inability to sleep directly paralleled his mother's experience in the Auschwitz concentration camp. He had always felt that someone was going to "get him" if he relaxed and closed his eyes, although he never knew why.

In his constellation, we explored the subtle and not-so-subtle dynamics of victim and perpetrator between his mother and the SS guards, allowing her experience with them to be just that — her experience, not Bob's. We finished the Constellation by honoring her fate and destiny, thereby acknowledging her strength and her ability to carry her own fate, without any help from the son she would have those many years later.

Not surprisingly, Bob started sleeping easily soon after. The horrors of WWII had finally been laid to rest in the past. And as Charlie Chaplin showed in his courageous film against the global insanity of Adolph Hitler, *The Great Dictator*, had been just a ruse. The Jewish heart, the Jewish soul, the Jewish spirit are still very much alive. And now Bob can feel that in every cell of his Jewish body.

38.

GETTING BEYOND
YOUR BACKSTORY

Now that you understand you are on a trajectory, it is time to clean up what came before. Believe it or not your subconscious journey from your family of origin has a lot to do with where you are now. To manifest your "Star Power" in the movie of your life we have to look back to go forward. To get you to the pinnacle of success and beyond we must take stock of where you came from. This will allow and empower you to create the life you desire and deserve.

As explained earlier in this book, your life follows a script and in this script there are a million scenes and stories that were in existence long before your arrival. Things can get convoluted along the way. Beliefs created by the need to survive pass on from generation to generation. The good news is that it worked. The bad news is that those beliefs do not necessarily hold up now. We carry the unfinished dramas and traumas out of love and for that sense of belonging in our family. There are plenty of good things, but, as we all know too well, there is a price and heavy baggage attached to the gifts.

Consciously parents and families want the best for their children. However, that powerful silent movie runs in the subconscious of every person. This is your unique "Family Movie". This secret movie can be so strong that it prevents you from creating your own script. Using Constellation Healing Experience to examine and disentangle yourself in a positive way can lead you to a place of empowerment - one where the "Family Movie" does not have so much control.

You are not your family but are from your family. You owe them respect and honor but the gift of life is yours to do as you please. You do not have to pay a price for being you or making your dreams come true.

Constellation Healing Experiences are a great way to access the deepest reaches of consciousness contained within you and your family system. This amazing process delves into the darkest and heaviest hours of family members whether present or past. The Constellation Field may seem stagnant or heavy at first. We are dredging up many old pains and wounds from battles long gone. The epigenetic effect still lingers in the client and in their family field. When released clients report feeling restored, rejuvenated, happier, with increased joy and well-being.

The more emotionally happy we are, the better our physical bodies and minds function, giving us the strength to live in a way that supports our ever-evolving needs. We continue to encounter challenges, but we will be able to face them with new resolve and resilience.

The goal of Constellation work is not to relieve the burden that family systems pass down from generation to generation but to transform it from being heavy to being light. It makes living so much better. What better legacy to leave than to be a happy, healthy person as an example for others?

39.
LOYALTY

Loyalty or lack there-of may be the single and biggest force that invisibly ties everyone to functional or dysfunctional family systems. There is comfort and familiarity in what is known and supported by family members and ancestors. Loyalty is the flip side of betrayal. Everyone wants to belong and is expected to toe the line as the price to belong. Those who do not or dance to the beat of their own drum are considered "disloyal" and treated as the "black sheep" of the family system. Those designated as being different in some way are perceived as "disloyal." They pay a heavy price for their desire to do things differently.

The status quo of generations has set strong rules of order to keep everyone identifying with their name and place in society. There can be great emphasis on tradition as well. The family can keep dark and dirty secrets. Any individual who speaks up can be viewed as the enemy or betrayer. They risk rejection for their honesty and will in most cases pay a price. Guilt and shame are powerful tools to manipulate and keep everyone in order and quiet. Everyone wants to belong and feeling excluded on an emotional level can feel like death. It takes tremendous courage and strength to go against the grain and express yourself in a different way than the rest of your family. Others in the family may ostracize and reject anyone who doesn't remain loyal and follow the family rules. Inclusion feels good and exclusion feels bad.

In families loyalty holds both tremendous power and tremendous conflict. The first inner conflict begins with loyalty to Mother and Father and their family systems. If a child was an accident or unwanted, the child will pick that up from the parents. It is a winning situation because the child receives life. It is also a losing situation because there is a huge emotional toll felt by the child. Hence the child will have an inner conflict around belonging its whole life and that is just over conception. The child conflict can spill into a feeling of not fitting into either the mother's or father's family system.

The deepest truth is when you are born you automatically belong to your family system. This birthright cannot be taken away. Your connection to the family may be tenuous but it exists. The experience can be filled with emotions of guilt, shame betrayal, grief, and loss. These emotions can cause you to act out. These behaviors may not be accepted by the family. It is up to your individuated spirit and courageousness to find the path through the labyrinth of the confines of your family system. Typically if you obey the family rules and behaviors you are accepted. Disobey and you will be ostracized.

To refine these dynamics more on a personal level it becomes our internal battle for personal integrity and autonomy over collective approval. The cruelest irony is that we belong to the family even if we betray their values. Betrayal and loyalty are some of the most complex rules people encounter. These dynamics also extend beyond family to work, friendships, romantic relationships, virtually every aspect life. Your behavior can be viewed positively or negatively by others. The acceptance or rejection of any group of people can happen at any time.

The huge conundrum you face is staying loyal to your

personal truth versus your need to belong with the others. You are always at choice. Should you be loyal to others even if it means suffering at a great personal loss? Are you willing to be shunned if you are not loyal to the family or group? You must decide if you can be strong enough to follow your truth even if it goes against the system. It is always your choice even if it is not always an easy one.

Ask yourself these questions:

- Who are you loyal to and why?

- Do you pay a price for this loyalty?

- What is that price?

- Are you loyal to yourself?

- Do you pay a price for that personal integrity?

- How do you handle these dynamics of loyalty and betrayal internally with family, socially, in business or other personal relationships?

- Are you unhappy about being perceived as betraying anyone by putting yourself first?

- Do you feel guilt for being who you are?

- How do you handle blame and possible shunning from others over your choices?

The interesting thing about loyalty and betrayal is how guilt and shame are used to keep you in line from a very young age. Organized, commercialized religion has capitalized on this to a "T" for centuries. They have the supreme guilt of God judging you if you do not follow orders. You must pay for forgiveness and absolution if you waver from the rules of these "Merchants of Dogma."

Those who choose to disagree strongly with any social

system also have the power to create an evolution of consciousness for the group that represses them. As we've discussed, Martin Luther King Jr.'s stance on civil rights and equality reverberate even more strongly today. He had the courage to address the racist attitudes of the white society he had to live in. He was accused of disloyalty by the government as he upended the status quo. He paid a steep price (his life) in doing so. His dream lives on even as the fight for equality and justice continues to rage from his ground breaking efforts over fifty years ago.

Christopher Columbus stayed loyal to his belief that the world was round when everyone else believed the world was flat. Society was loyal to their ignorance even while Columbus was loyal to his search for proof. He was betraying the status quo by staying loyal to his vision. Society remained loyal to their beliefs until Columbus returned with the proof. At that point, society turned its back on its previous belief and became loyal to Columbus' proof that the world was indeed round and not flat.

Mahatma Gandhi said, "First they ignore you, then they laugh at you, then they fight you, then you win." It is really the dynamics of the macrocosm of life in a microcosm on many, many levels. This is true in families. There are millions of examples including you and your family system of origin. Is there loyalty to a perpetrator or loyalty to victims? There are prices for silence and for speaking up.

As noted previously there is a theory that the amount of cancer that is raging today is caused by the unspoken secrets. The silent victims get sick and die, possibly out of fear of being disloyal. It may also be alive in the perpetrator who cannot live with him or herself over those he or she victimized. There is always a price to pay either way. No one escapes anything. Your family system is a microcosm of the world. There are prices to pay internally or externally. Every person on this earth is affected by the invisible and dynamics.

If you feel trapped there is a way out. Constellations are one readily available process that can give you an overview of your place in the family system as well a tangible opportunity to heal it.

40.

LIFE PATH:
YOUR HERO'S JOURNEY

Every good story needs a hero or heroine to root for; someone to uplift and inspire the audience. Any story, whether it is an ancient Greek myth, an 18th century novel or a contemporary film, has the same elements. The most basic is the protagonist. When we watch the story through the eyes of this main character we want this person to win as they struggle against on ore more antagonists. Ironically, the conflict between these characters is what causes growth.

During the holidays the classic *It's a Wonderful Life* airs non-stop. In this brilliant, timeless film we see a poignant juxtaposition of opposing outcomes; how life manifests if the antagonist wins versus if the protagonist comes out on top. In one plot line Mr. Potter, a wealthy banker, puts money and his own greedy self-interest above that of the community, thereby creating his own "Potterville Hell." The community is sadly defeated. Life is dreary.

Conversely, the story unfolds quite differently after an angel shows the main character George how this hellish life would have been created if he had not been alive to stop it. He chooses in that moment to live. Not only does he live with gusto, but he redoubles his efforts to do good for others. His attitude shift and belief that he makes a difference has the audience cheering for him. He is rewarded with a life full of love, family, and a dear friend that help him in what could have been his darkest hour.

Most of us identify with the hero. We want to be like George, fighting injustice. In every movie from *Indiana Jones* to *Rocky*, from *The Lone Ranger* to *The Matrix*, the hero is cut from the same cloth. We rally for those who can beat the odds, win, and vanquish the oppressors. Now let us go deeper and dissect the dynamics that create the hero. The antagonist creates conflict. The struggle convinces the protagonist to rise to the occasion and achieve greatness. For it to work we need both characters because "it takes two to tango." We can't know light without dark or dark without light. They are flip sides of the same coin. The antagonist acts as a catalyst, helping the protagonist to find his or her inner strength and develop into the hero.

In every film or movie just as in your life, conflicts create the story. We identify with the hero and route for him or her to win. We see the hero as the star and are looking at the world through that character's eyes. If you look at your own life as a movie, don't you want to be the hero too – not just an extra? However, are you playing your real heroic role? Are you the main character but playing the role of a victim where everything is done to you? Are you the antagonist? Or are you a protagonist who is in the midst of overcoming?

Your training ground for these dramas occurred during your formative years mostly with your family. Some were protagonists and some were antagonists. All of them influence you, even the ones you have not met. Remember that both protagonists and antagonists are needed for growth. It is the adversarial dynamic that contributes to the evolution of life. You need "yin" to experience "yang." Antagonists are necessary to inspire the protagonist to gain strength and grow. Both are important for balance and transformation.

Most people in life are so distracted by problems, dramas and traumas that they most often fail to see their strengths. More often than not your training is happening behind the scenes on a subconscious level unbeknownst to you during the events. The major players, both antagonistic and protagonist, are people in your family. However you were also affected by social relationships with neighbors, teachers, other families, and other children.

The biggest irony is that it is not often the other person's intention to be an antagonist. They are living their own movie and have other influences in their lives. Using your "Power of Presence" helps you put some distance between yourself and the emotional roller coaster you may be experiencing. Then you begin to sort it all out.

PART SIX

ACTIVATE NOW!

41.
PROSPERITY CONSTELLATIONS

The desire for success is universal. Whether it is in the competitive business world or simply within our own personal lives, we all hope to be the best we can be. Yet far too often, we feel at a loss as to how to attain the level of success we want. So often we feel we are at the mercy of outside forces rather than in control of our own destiny.

No one could have felt less in control of his life than I did. I was a child of poverty, physical abuse, and my father died when I was very young. It seemed that my past had given me so many negatives to focus on that I carried those feelings of failure with me well into my adulthood. Then I discovered a way to view the past much differently than I ever had before. I discovered a modality known as Constellation work, and it has changed my life forever.

I want to share the steps I took many years ago on my journey from feeling like the ultimate victim to feeling like the ultimate success. Ironically, that had not been my goal. I had simply hoped to find happiness in spite of the odds being stacked against me. After doing some Constellation work, I began to realize more than just a sense of well-being; I realized how I had been keeping myself stuck in a cycle of failure and subtle self-sabotage. It was up to me to change what I had into what I wanted.

I became a fully-accredited, double-certified Constellation facilitator nearly two decades ago. Since then, I have learned many valuable lessons on how to change from self-sabotaging to self-actualizing. There are certain mental and behavioral patterns we continue to repeat even though those patterns do not serve us. There are some simple, proactive steps you can take to help you not only recognize such patterns but empower you to break them. However, before you can move forward, you need to look back.

Step 1. Consider Your Connection to the Past

It is amazing how often people will expect to get different results without changing their actions. One thing that makes a person successful is the ability to learn from mistakes. Instead of seeing mistakes as negative, we should see that mistakes are actually gifts.

Allegedly negative events can strengthen our resolve, affording us the opportunity to develop better problem solving skills. For years I was so trapped in my own "Shoulda, Coulda, Woulda" mind set, I was failing to see that I could harness the same energy I was expending wallowing in "what wasn't" and use it to work toward "what can be." I realized that being stuck in a rut of dissatisfaction was a choice, and I was ready to choose something different.

Taking stock of my personal and professional experiences, I began to see that the past had a strong impact on me. It was not just my past, but my family's past too. I discovered that along with my family history, I also inherited an emotional blueprint from my ancestors which affected how I dealt with the various challenges I faced in my life. I too felt an unspoken loyalty to those who came before, and a feeling that it was up to me to right their wrongs. I sometimes limited my success so

I wouldn't do "better" than they did.

These kind of subconscious connections are known as "entanglements." They can affect us much more than we realize. Our families' habits and patterns developed as reactions to times and situations that no longer exists. Yet out of love and loyalty, we tend to mimic their perspectives and perpetuate their reactions even though doing so may not be serving us and, in fact, may be sabotaging our success.

But how do we break the pattern? How do we reconcile the guilt we feel if we dare to be prosperous when they were not? And how can we overcome this fear of betrayal that keeps us from taking matters into our own hands? Believe it or not, the answer lies in acceptance.

Step 2. Transform Your Perception of the Past

As the old adage goes, "Those who don't learn from the past are doomed to repeat it." If I have learned one thing from my sixty-plus years on this earth, it is just how very true this is. When we consider how much we are shaped by not only our own experiences but by our familial examples as well, it is so important that we recognize the gift in those experiences as well.

The worst thing we could do is to push the past away. When we say, "I am nothing like my mother," or "I will never be like my father," we are actually denying ourselves a very necessary and empowering connection to our creators. Our family is a source of support. We would not be here without them. When we exclude them, we exclude a part of ourselves.

Empowerment requires wholeness. That is why every facet needs to be seen and included — the good, the bad and the ugly. In order for us to break a pattern, we must first be willing to acknowledge its existence. Only then can we make the conscious choice to do things differently.

When I set out on my own healing path at a young age, I had no idea I was actually on my way to becoming a healing practitioner. My only intention was to heal myself. I wanted to grow and learn as much about my own internal process as I possibly could. In hindsight I realize I was already developing the personal empowerment techniques I use and share today in my lectures and Constellation workshops. We are all being guided by forces larger than ourselves. I see now that my past experiences were actually the fodder for my yet unrealized future. I would never know the level of empowerment or support I have from my past if I had not chosen to change my negative perception of it.

Look at the choices you make, and consider what drives those decisions. Obstacles and challenges are teaching tools. Think of the possible outcomes before you implement any changes so that you can be empowered by your own objectivity. The world actually encourages us more than we realize. Each step brings another gift. The question is, are we open to receiving them?

The gift of the past is experience, both our own as well as that of others. The gift of the present is choice: Do we let the past entangle us or support us in moving forward? When we can come from a place of acceptance rather than rejection, we are free to make different choice. That will lead to different results.

Step 3. Be Willing To Leave it in the Past

Our connections to the past are strong, but patterns can be broken and perceptions can be altered. When we are feeling stuck or at a loss as to how to proceed, we are actually demonstrating our loyalty to our established mode of operation. It is scary to try something new. Comfort zones only limit our greater success. We need to let go of what does not work in order to make room for what will.

The Constellation process helps us pinpoint the specific aspects that are entanglements. It highlights what we need to disengage from (or better still, transform into support) in order to move forward. Having gone through my own experience, I know the process inside out, and I can help guide you along every liberating step of the way.

It is seeing these dynamics from a different perspective that allows us to understand the deeper truths about what may be blocking us from greater success. Once we are aware of them, they can no longer exert their power in unseen ways. This frees us from any energetic hold they may have had. Simply put, the work brings objectivity to our subjective beliefs.

We all take on burdens that are not actually ours to carry. Constellations can help us distinguish what is and what is not ours. They afford us the opportunity to harness the power of the past in new and empowering ways. They make those previously unseen dynamics that have been adversely affecting our ability to move forward, visible.

We come away with a conscience free of guilt or shame because we attain a deeper understanding that we share the same dream of prosperity and fulfillment with those who came before. When it comes true for us, it comes true for them. We no longer need to carry anything for them. Their fate was theirs, and they can carry it. When we acknowledge their strength, we can acknowledge our own, and we are free.

The road to success does not have to be a long and winding one. There are simple yet profound steps you can take to help you move forward into a prosperous and unencumbered future. Learn from your experiences. See that even the most negative ones still hold valuable lessons.

It is your future. Let it come with the gift of empowerment. Take control of your own destiny, and shape it however you see fit, both personally and professionally. You deserve success. You deserve happiness. You can have both.

42.
CONSTELLATION HEALING FAQS

Systemic ancestral, family and organizational Constellations reveal and release hidden dynamics that cause entanglements. These energetic, unconscious obstacles affect our health, career and interpersonal relationships.

What is a Constellation?

Subconscious bonds and deep loyalties exist in every aspect of our lives. Constellations tap into this "Conscious Field of Totality and reveal unseen aspects that may have a negative effect in our lives.

Our unconscious becomes conscious, allowing us the freedom to make healthy choices, allowing us to make a change. We can rewrite the future script of our lives in a new, positive, and empowering way.

How does it work?

Through the use of representatives to access hidden dynamics, we gain objectivity and transformation. Witnessing the subtle dimensions that each problem contains actually transforms the energy and allows resolution.

What happens in a Constellation?

In a group setting a client chooses to work on a goal they want to achieve in their life in an area where they feel stuck. The only other person in the room that knows their family history is the facilitator.

The other people in the workshop are participants and may choose their level of participation. Some may choose to observe only. Others choose to volunteer as representative. They may represent an person, problem or thing for the client.

When the Constellation begins the client chooses one person to represent themselves. They think of their goal as they stand behind their representative and touch their shoulders. The representative then describes feelings or physical sensations that come up for them. The facilitator adds other people into the Constellation who function as other elements in the story. The representatives usually do not know anything about the people or family yet are able to react to each other with positive or negative feelings. The airing of these familial aspects opens up positive energy and a ripe environment for the client's goal to flourish. Constellation work can also be done from a distance. The power of the field can change a dynamic in a client's life even if they are thousands of miles away.

What are possible Constellation goals?

Constellations can help with issues of money, health, work, grief and loss, sexuality, phobias, relationships and intimacy, anger, divorce, adoption, any number of areas that could use improvement. Disentangling ourselves from the ghosts of the past allows us to move forward into the future we want to live in.

Who ya gonna call? *Ghostbusters*? *The Exorcist*? No, all you need to do to free yourself from what hasn't been working is to allow yourself a different perspective on why you do what you do. And I can help you do just that.

43.

IN CONCLUSION

Every script begins as a blank page, and my story was no different. When I started out on my healing path those many, many years ago, I only knew I desired freedom and happiness, yet felt trapped as an extra in a movie not of my own making. I had a childhood that made *American Horror Story* look like a picnic. Later, in the 70's, I entered into popular encounter groups that made *One Flew Over the Cuckoo's Nest* look like *Rebecca of Sunnybrook Farm*. Then it was off to Primal Scream Therapy, but that was too *Truth or Dare* for my taste. At least it allowed me to find my voice, and it did blow the lid off of my emotional repression. After all, I learned I was not *Despicable Me* but merely at the effect of my sibling minions.

Act One and Act Two of my life were more like *Scream* and *Scream 2*. The good news is I was on my way out of the *Twilight Zone* of my own dysfunctional home movie. Discovering Bert Hellinger's Constellation Healing Work was the best thing that could have ever happened to me. He, like any good director, helped me see the deeper motivations behind the painful scenes and the drama that had been my life. Somehow it allowed me to develop a *Sixth Sense* to play back those scenes in a new way, objectively and without judgment, giving me a deeper love for my fate with my family, and a newfound strength that took me beyond the perceived suffering.

Like a phoenix rising out of the ashes, I went from *Misery* to *A Star is Born*. After decades of self-discovery, the time came for me to shine. Looking back, I realize now that I had always deserved to be the author of my own story and the star of my own life. And that goes for all of us. You don't need to wait another minute. You can create the life you want to live right now, from this day forward, *From Here To Eternity*. And be willing to trust in your own vision enough that you're willing to leave whatever doesn't work on the cutting room floor. The old melodramas of the past may have been necessary to get you to where you are now, but continuing to replay them may be blocking the true and deeper movie from coming through. Remember, *Whose Life Is It Anyway?*

We all have the capability to write, direct, and star in our own lives. So why not create the story that serves us best? *One Life to Live* was a soap opera, not a feature film. Do you want to be mired in drama, or the hero of your own life mission? This is your chance. This is your story. The production will wrap soon enough. Let's make it count before we …

Fade to Black.

PART SEVEN

Afterword

44.
ABOUT THE AUTHOR

Gary Stuart has been exploring invisible family dynamics as a Constellation facilitator for more than 16 years. Double-certified, his first certification was completed during Heinz Stark's first U.S. facilitator training in 2000-2002. While continuing his weekly workshops, Gary then completed Bert Hellinger's first "Movements of the Spirit-Mind" training in Pichl, Austria in 2007.

Having facilitated well over 8,000 processes, he is now a leader in the field, applying the modality to prosperity challenges, familial and epigenetic dynamics, as well as exploring past-life and re-incarnational issues. He conducts workshops in Los Angeles as well as other cities in the U.S. and internationally, employing a humorous, joyful, signature style he refers to as "Spirited Constellations."

Gary also offers "Distance Constellations" for both personal and organizational empowerment. His inspirational training program for budding facilitators is recognized in the US and internationally.

He founded the Constellation Healing Institute (C.H.I.) in 2008, and released *Many Hearts, One Soul* which speaks to the spiritual aspects behind the ground breaking modality of systemic constellation work. He is a regular contributor to *The Knowing Field* in the UK, and has also has authored four other books on various spiritual and philosophical subjects.

He is a member of the ISCA, Hellinger Sciencia, the Holistic Chamber of Commerce, and The Evolutionary Business Council.

45.

MY SUPPORTING CAST OF CHARACTERS

Tremendous gratitude to the following cast members:

The man behind the curtain:
Gary Corb

Foreword:
Robert Clancy
www.guidetothesoul.com

Cover art, interior book design:
Ellen Perry
www.ellenperry.com

Content and flow:
Kathryn LaBarbera

Special thanks to:
Teresa de Grosbois
Shawne Duperon
Ellen Rogin
Kelly Carlin
Colin Sprake
Debbie Dachinger

46.

YOUR TICKET TO SUCCESS

ere's your opportunity to join Gary Stuart's **Constellation Healing Community**. Get ongoing transformational support from a master facilitator. Build on what you learned in *Master Your Universe*. Experience for yourself the profound impact your ancestral history has on your current family system.

> Consult with Gary and discover how
> Constellation Healing Experience
> can help you and your family.
>
> Contact Gary:
> (800) 361-2692
> Gary@MasterYourUniverseBook.com
>
> For more info visit
> www.masteryouruniversebook.com

Imagine the relief you'll feel when you get unstuck. You'll begin to see things that were once negative in a more positive, empowering light. Let Gary guide you into a new awareness through the power of Constellation Healing.